christmas
FEASTS and TREATS

Fourth Estate
An imprint of HarperCollins*Publishers*

First published in Australia and New Zealand in 2018
by HarperCollins*Publishers* Australia Pty Limited
ABN 36 009 913 517   harpercollins.com.au

HarperCollins*Publishers*
Level 13, 201 Elizabeth Street, Sydney NSW 2000, Australia
Unit D1, 63 Apollo Drive, Rosedale, Auckland 0632, New Zealand
A 53, Sector 57, Noida, UP, India
1 London Bridge Street, London SE1 9GF, United Kingdom
Bay Adelaide Centre, East Tower, 22 Adelaide Street West, 41st floor, Toronto, Ontario M5H 4E3, Canada
195 Broadway, New York NY 10007, USA

A catalogue record for this book is available from the National Library of Australia
ISBN: 978 1 4607 5780 2

On the cover: gingerbread cookie, photographed by William Meppem

Reproduction by News PreMedia Centre
Printed and bound in China by RR Donnelley on 157gsm Golden Sun Matt Art and 140gsm Golden Sun Woodfree
6 5 4 3 2   19 20 21

christmas
FEASTS and TREATS

FOURTH ESTATE

contents

feasts
pages 8 – 113

HOW TO COOK
ham *page 26*
turkey *page 36*
pork *page 58*
lobster *page 70*
parsnips *page 78*

QUICK FIX
nibbles *page 16*
sides *page 100*

treats
pages 114 – 225

HOW TO COOK
christmas cake *page 116*
christmas pudding *page 128*
trifle *page 160*
fruit mince pies *page 186*
shortbread *page 198*
gingerbread *page 212*

QUICK FIX
nougat *page 178*
candy canes *page 196*
cookies *page 210*
edible decorations *page 220*

glossary and index
pages 226 – 239

introduction

Christmas at my house usually consists of my
three favourite things – family, laughter and,
let's be honest, a little craziness. My boys wake up
super early (of course!) so, after a few presents,
it's become a ritual of ours to dash down for a swim
in the ocean. Refreshed and salty, we head home
to get ready for lunch, and it's not long before I'm
prepping canapés in the kitchen with my sisters and
a glass of Champagne. It's these kinds of moments
I think we all treasure on Christmas Day. Don't
get me wrong, I have quite the weakness for festive
food and all its trimmings, but I'm also really into
finding new ways to dial down the entertaining
stress and make more room for fun. This book
has all my fuss-free tips, styling tricks and, most
importantly, stunning but simple recipes you can
count on for the big day. It's my way of wishing
you a very happy (and relaxed!) Christmas.

feasts

I know some of you celebrate with an enchanting dinner on Christmas Eve, and some will be hosting a long lunch on the day itself. Maybe you're a guest this year and you've been asked to bring something? You'll find all things savoury to feast on here. There's inspiration for starters and sides, plus step-by-step guides to walk you through the big four: glazed ham, succulent turkey, roast pork and grilled lobster. Keep an eye out for my tips and shortcuts, like my glossy cheat's ham that doesn't require basting every 10 minutes, and turkey that cooks gently on the stovetop (in less than an hour!), leaving room for ham and vegetables in the oven below.

onion, brie and rosemary tarts

onion, brie and rosemary tarts

40g unsalted butter
3 onions, thinly sliced
1 tablespoon caster (superfine) sugar
2 tablespoons white wine vinegar
¼ cup rosemary leaves
sea salt and cracked black pepper
3 sheets frozen shortcrust pastry, thawed
¾ cup (180ml) single (pouring) cream
3 eggs, lightly beaten
¼ teaspoon finely grated nutmeg
150g brie, cut into 12 slices
12 x 4cm-long sprigs rosemary, extra, to serve

Preheat oven to 200°C (400°F). Melt the butter in a large
non-stick frying pan over medium heat. Add the onion, cover
with a tight-fitting lid and cook for 10 minutes. Add the sugar,
vinegar, rosemary, salt and pepper and cook, uncovered, for
5 minutes or until the onion is golden brown.

Lightly grease 12 x ⅓-cup-capacity (80ml) muffin tins.
Using a 10cm round cutter, cut 12 rounds from the pastry and
use them to line the tins. Prick the bases with a fork. Divide the
onion mixture between the pastry cases. Place the cream, eggs,
nutmeg, salt and pepper in a medium jug and whisk to combine.
Pour cream mixture into each case and top with a slice of brie.

Bake for 20–25 minutes or until the pastry is golden and the
egg is just set. Allow to cool in the tins for 5 minutes before
placing onto wire racks. Top each tart with the extra rosemary
to serve. MAKES 12

earl grey, gin and tarragon gravlax

1kg rock salt
2 cups (440g) white (granulated) sugar
⅓ cup (25g) earl grey tea leaves
2 tablespoons finely grated lemon rind
⅓ cup tarragon leaves, finely chopped
½ cup (125ml) gin
1 x 1kg side sashimi-grade trout, skin on and pin-boned
store-bought lavosh crackers or flatbreads, to serve
crème fraîche, to serve
cornichons or pickled onions, to serve
black sea salt flakes, to serve

Place the salt, sugar, tea leaves, lemon rind, tarragon and gin
in a large bowl and mix to combine. Place 2 sheets of plastic
wrap on a large baking tray, overlapping to make them large
enough to cover the fish. Spread the tray with half the salt
mixture and top with the trout, skin-side down. Top with the
remaining salt mixture and wrap tightly in the plastic wrap.
Top with a second baking tray and weigh down with 2–3 cans
or a heavy saucepan. Refrigerate for 36 hours, turning the
fish every 12 hours.

Remove the fish from the plastic wrap, rinse off the salt
mixture and pat dry with absorbent kitchen paper. Using a
sharp knife, thinly slice the fish from the skin. Serve with
crackers, crème fraîche, cornichons and sea salt. SERVES 8-10
Tip: The cured fish will keep refrigerated, tightly covered in plastic
wrap, for up to 3 days.

earl grey, gin and tarragon gravlax

smoky barbecued prawns

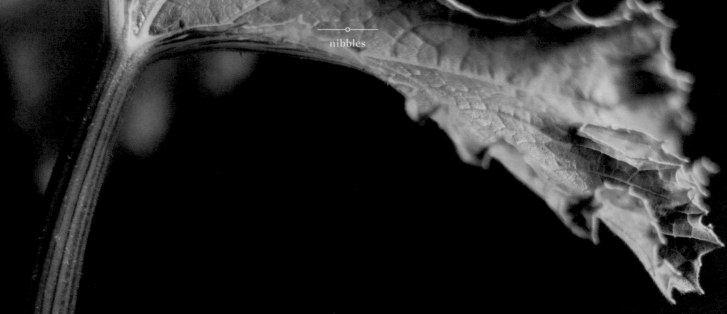

smoky barbecued prawns

1kg green (raw) king prawns (shrimp)[+], shells intact
smoky barbecue butter
200g unsalted butter, softened
1 teaspoon tomato paste
1½ teaspoons cayenne pepper
2 teaspoons smoked paprika
2 teaspoons ground sumac
1 teaspoon Worcestershire sauce
1 teaspoon honey
2 teaspoons mustard powder
2 cloves garlic, crushed
sea salt and cracked black pepper

To make the smoky barbecue butter, place the butter, tomato paste, cayenne pepper, paprika, sumac, Worcestershire sauce, honey, mustard, garlic, salt and pepper in a bowl and whisk to combine. Reserve and set aside half the butter.

Thread the prawns onto bamboo skewers. Preheat a chargrill pan or barbecue over high heat. Add the skewers and cook for 2 minutes, brushing with the butter. Turn and cook, brushing with any extra butter, for a further 1–2 minutes or until cooked through. Sprinkle the prawns with salt and pepper and serve with the reserved butter. SERVES 4-6
+ These large, succulent prawns have a rich flavour and are delicious freshly barbecued, crumbed and fried, or used in seafood soups.

crab, ricotta and tarragon stuffed zucchini flowers

150g cooked picked crab meat[+]
¾ cup (180g) fresh firm ricotta
2 teaspoons finely grated lemon rind
2 tablespoons finely chopped tarragon
1 teaspoon sea salt flakes, plus extra for sprinkling
16 zucchini (courgette) flowers
vegetable oil, for deep frying
2 tablespoons self-raising (self-rising) flour
lemon wedges, to serve
batter
1 cup (150g) cornflour (cornstarch)
½ cup (75g) self-raising (self-rising) flour
1¾ cups (430ml) iced water

To make the batter, place the cornflour, flour and water in a large bowl and mix using a butter knife until just combined but still lumpy. Allow to stand for 10 minutes.

Place the crab, ricotta, lemon rind, tarragon and salt in a medium bowl and mix to combine. Spoon into a piping bag fitted with a 1cm round nozzle and pipe the mixture into each zucchini flower, twisting the petals to enclose.

Half-fill a large saucepan with oil and place over medium heat until it reaches 180°C (350°F) on a deep-frying thermometer. In batches, dust the zucchini flowers in the flour, dip in the batter and cook for 2–3 minutes or until golden. Drain on absorbent kitchen paper, sprinkle with salt and serve with lemon wedges. SERVES 4
+ You can buy cooked picked crab meat from your fishmonger.

crab, ricotta and tarragon stuffed zucchini flowers

smoked salmon, wasabi and radish finger sandwiches

250g cream cheese, softened
2 teaspoons wasabi paste
2 teaspoons finely grated lime rind
8 thick slices white bread
4 radishes (150g), trimmed and thinly sliced
8 slices (250g) smoked salmon
micro (baby) shiso leaves (optional), to serve
cracked black pepper, to serve

Place the cream cheese, wasabi and lime rind in a small
bowl and mix to combine.

Spread two-thirds of the mixture onto the bread slices.
Cover 4 of the bread slices with the radish and top with the
remaining bread, cream cheese-side down. Spread the top
of each sandwich with the remaining cream cheese mixture.
Place 2 slices of the salmon on each sandwich. Trim the
crusts and slice each sandwich into 3 lengths.

Sprinkle with shiso leaves and pepper to serve. **MAKES 12**

smoked salmon, mascarpone and tarragon pâté

1 cup (250g) mascarpone
⅓ cup tarragon leaves
1 tablespoon Dijon mustard
1 teaspoon finely grated lemon rind
1 tablespoon lemon juice
cracked black pepper, for sprinkling
300g smoked salmon, chopped
salmon roe, to serve
store-bought seeded crackers, to serve

Place the mascarpone, tarragon, mustard, lemon rind, lemon
juice and pepper in a food processor and process until smooth.
Add the salmon and pulse until just combined. Divide between
serving bowls or sterilised jars and top with salmon roe.

Serve the pâté with seeded crackers. **SERVES 6**
Tip: This pâté will keep refrigerated for 2–3 days.

prawns with bloody mary mayonnaise and celery salt

1kg cooked prawns (shrimp), shells intact
celery salt+, to serve
bloody mary mayonnaise
1 cup (300g) whole-egg mayonnaise
2 teaspoons Tabasco sauce
2 teaspoons Worcestershire sauce
1½ tablespoons tomato sauce (ketchup)
sea salt and cracked black pepper
2 stalks celery, trimmed and finely chopped

To make the bloody mary mayonnaise, place the mayonnaise, Tabasco, Worcestershire sauce, tomato sauce, salt and pepper in a small bowl and mix to combine. Top with the celery.

Place the prawns on a serving plate, sprinkle with the celery salt and serve with the bloody mary mayonnaise. SERVES 4
+ *Find celery salt in supermarkets or make your own with 1 teaspoon celery seeds and 1 tablespoon sea salt flakes.*
Tip: You can serve the prawns on a bed of crushed ice, if you like.

spicy tabasco lobster sliders

¼ teaspoon dried chilli flakes
1 teaspoon sea salt flakes
¼ cup (75g) whole-egg mayonnaise
2 tablespoons tomato sauce (ketchup)
1 teaspoon Tabasco sauce
1 teaspoon Worcestershire sauce
300g cooked lobster meat, chopped
8 small brioche slider buns, halved
micro (baby) mint leaves (optional), to serve

Place the chilli and salt in a small bowl, mix to combine and set aside.

Place the mayonnaise, tomato sauce, Tabasco, Worcestershire sauce and lobster in a medium bowl and mix to combine. Divide the lobster mixture between the bun bases, top with the mint and sprinkle with the chilli salt. Sandwich with the bun tops to serve. MAKES 8
+ *You can buy cooked lobster meat or lobster tails from your fishmonger.*

ginger, soy and mirin oysters

¼ cup (60ml) mirin (Japanese rice wine)
2 teaspoons soy sauce
1 teaspoon sesame oil
1 tablespoon rice wine vinegar
1 teaspoon lime juice
1 teaspoon finely grated ginger
12 oysters, freshly shucked
black sesame seeds, toasted, to serve
micro (baby) shiso leaves (optional)[+], to serve
lime wedges, to serve

Place the mirin, soy, sesame oil, vinegar, lime juice
and ginger in a small bowl and whisk to combine.
   Place the oysters on a serving plate and spoon
the dressing on top. Sprinkle with the sesame seeds
and shiso and serve with lime wedges. MAKES 12
+ *Micro herbs are available from greengrocers, farmers'
markets and some supermarkets.*
*Tip: You can serve the oysters on a bed of crushed ice,
if you like.*

tarragon crab cakes with aioli

500g cooked picked crab meat[+]
1½ cups (100g) fresh sourdough breadcrumbs
1 teaspoon finely grated lemon rind
2 tablespoons finely chopped flat-leaf parsley
2 tablespoons finely chopped tarragon
¼ cup (75g) aioli, plus extra to serve
sea salt and cracked black pepper
¼ cup (60ml) vegetable oil
watercress sprigs, to serve

Place the crab, breadcrumbs, lemon rind, parsley, tarragon,
aioli, salt and pepper in a large bowl and mix well to combine.
Shape ⅓-cup portions of the mixture into patties.
   Heat the oil in a large non-stick frying pan over medium
heat. Cook the crab cakes in batches for 3 minutes each
side or until golden and crisp. Sprinkle with pepper and
serve with watercress and extra aioli. MAKES 8
+ *You can buy cooked picked crab meat from your fishmonger.*

ricotta and pea tartlets

6 small flatbreads
2 tablespoons extra virgin olive oil, for brushing
2 cups (480g) fresh firm ricotta
1 teaspoon finely grated lemon rind
sea salt and cracked black pepper
1 cup (120g) frozen peas, blanched
1 cup snow pea (mange tout) tendrils

Preheat oven to 180°C (350°F). Using an 11cm round cutter, cut 6 rounds from the flatbreads and gently peel to separate each round in half. Brush both sides of the flatbreads with the oil and press in to line 12 x ½-cup-capacity (125ml) muffin tins. Bake for 4–6 minutes or until crisp and golden. Allow to cool in the tins for 5 minutes before removing.

Place the ricotta, lemon rind, salt and pepper in a medium bowl and mix to combine. Place the peas in a small bowl and gently mash with a fork.

Divide the ricotta mixture between the tartlets and top with the peas, snow pea tendrils, salt and pepper to serve. MAKES 12

smoked salmon and avocado rice paper rolls

8 x 16cm rice paper rounds
8 slices (250g) smoked salmon
1 carrot, peeled and shredded
1 cucumber, shredded
1 avocado, thinly sliced
½ cup coriander (cilantro) leaves
black sesame seeds, to serve
micro (baby) mint leaves (optional), to serve
store-bought pickled chilli[+], to serve

Place 1 rice paper round in a large bowl of warm water for 10 seconds to soften. Place on a clean surface and allow to stand for a further 5–10 seconds. Place 1 slice of the salmon in the centre of the round, top with a little of the carrot, cucumber, avocado and coriander and roll to enclose. Repeat with the remaining ingredients to make 8 rolls.

Cut the rolls in half and sprinkle with sesame seeds and mint. Serve with pickled chilli. MAKES 16
+ Pickled chilli is available from Asian supermarkets.

hummus with spiced crispy chickpeas

hummus with spiced crispy chickpeas

2 x 400g cans chickpeas (garbanzo beans), drained and rinsed
2 tablespoons tahini
1 clove garlic, crushed
⅓ cup (80ml) lemon juice
¼ cup (60ml) extra virgin olive oil, plus extra to serve
sea salt and cracked black pepper
2 tablespoons water
micro (baby) coriander (cilantro) leaves (optional)+, to serve
store-bought grissini (bread sticks), to serve
lemon wedges, to serve
spiced crispy chickpeas
¼ cup (50g) white rice flour
2 teaspoons smoked paprika, plus extra for sprinkling
2 teaspoons ground coriander
1 x 400g can chickpeas (garbanzo beans), drained and rinsed
vegetable oil, for shallow frying

Place the chickpeas, tahini, garlic, lemon juice, olive oil, salt and pepper in a food processor and process until smooth. Add the water to thin the hummus if necessary, processing to combine. Refrigerate for 1 hour or until chilled.

To make the spiced crispy chickpeas, place the flour, paprika and ground coriander in a medium bowl and mix to combine. Add the chickpeas and toss to coat. Heat 1cm of vegetable oil in a large non-stick frying pan over medium heat. Cook the chickpeas, in batches, for 4–5 minutes or until crisp and golden. Drain on absorbent kitchen paper and sprinkle with salt, pepper and the extra paprika.

Spoon the hummus onto a serving plate and top with the crispy chickpeas. Drizzle with extra oil, sprinkle with coriander leaves and pepper and serve with grissini and lemon wedges. **MAKES 2½ CUPS**

+ *Micro herbs are available from greengrocers, farmers' markets and some supermarkets.*

minted spinach dip with yoghurt

500g baby spinach leaves
½ cup (80g) natural almonds, toasted
3 cups mint leaves
1 tablespoon finely grated lemon rind
1 tablespoon lemon juice
sea salt and cracked black pepper
1 cup (280g) natural Greek-style (thick) yoghurt,
   plus extra to serve
2 tablespoons extra virgin olive oil
micro (baby) basil leaves (optional)+, to serve
store-bought lavosh crackers, to serve

Blanch the spinach, in batches, in a large saucepan of salted boiling water for 30 seconds – 1 minute or until wilted. Refresh in iced water and drain well.

Place the almonds in a food processor and process until fine. Add the spinach, mint, lemon rind and juice, salt and pepper and process until smooth. Add the yoghurt and oil and process to combine. Refrigerate for 1 hour or until chilled.

Spoon the dip onto a serving plate and top with extra yoghurt and basil leaves. Serve with crackers. **MAKES 3 CUPS**

+ *Micro herbs are available from greengrocers, farmers' markets and some supermarkets.*

minted spinach dip with yoghurt

tuna dip with dukkah

tuna dip with dukkah

1 x 185g can tuna in chilli oil, drained and oil reserved
3 white anchovy fillets
250g cream cheese, chopped
2 tablespoons lemon juice
2 tablespoons extra virgin olive oil
sea salt and cracked black pepper
store-bought dukkah+, for sprinkling
sourdough baguette, to serve
lemon wedges, to serve

Place the tuna, anchovies, cream cheese, lemon juice, olive oil, salt and pepper in a food processor and process, scraping down the sides of the bowl, for 3–4 minutes or until smooth. Refrigerate for 1 hour or until chilled.

Spoon the dip onto a serving plate, drizzle with the reserved chilli oil and sprinkle with dukkah. Serve with sourdough bread and lemon wedges. **MAKES 2½ CUPS**
+ Dukkah is a Middle-Eastern nut and spice blend, available from spice shops, delicatessens, greengrocers and most supermarkets. Sprinkle it on meats and salads or use it in a spice crust.

labne with pistachios and pomegranate

1 teaspoon sea salt flakes
1kg natural Greek-style (thick) yoghurt
2 tablespoons extra virgin olive oil, plus extra to serve
5 sprigs marjoram
seeds and juice from 1 pomegranate
2 tablespoons slivered pistachios
store-bought lavosh crackers or flatbreads, to serve

Add the salt to the yoghurt and mix to combine. Place in a bowl lined with a double layer of muslin and gather up the edges to enclose. Suspend the yoghurt from a shelf in the refrigerator, placing a bowl underneath to collect moisture, for 24 hours or until the mixture is firm. Unwrap the labne from the muslin and spoon onto a serving plate.

Heat the oil in a small non-stick frying pan over medium heat. Cook the marjoram, in batches, for 30 seconds – 1 minute or until just crispy. Drain on absorbent kitchen paper.

Drizzle the labne with the extra oil and 2 tablespoons of the pomegranate juice. Sprinkle with the pomegranate seeds and pistachios. Top with the crispy marjoram and serve with crackers. **MAKES 2½ CUPS**
Tips: Keep labne refrigerated in an airtight container for up to 1 week. When frying herbs in oil, make sure they are dry to start with – this will help prevent the oil from spitting.

labne with pistachios and pomegranate

score the rind

gently pull it back

remove the rind

wrap the hock

pour the glaze over the ham

cheat's glazed ham

3 cups (750ml) orange juice
3 cups (525g) light brown sugar
1 cup (250ml) red wine vinegar
1 stick cinnamon
8 cloves
16 sprigs thyme
3 cups (750ml) port
1 x 6–7kg ham leg+

Preheat oven to 220°C (425°F). Place the juice, sugar, vinegar, cinnamon, cloves and thyme in a medium saucepan over high heat and stir until the sugar has dissolved. Bring to the boil and cook for 30 minutes or until reduced. Remove from the heat, add the port and stir to combine. Strain the glaze into a heatproof jug, discarding the solids.

Use a sharp knife to score the skin around the sides and hock of the ham, before using your fingers to gently remove the rind. Trim any excess fat. Wrap the hock of the ham with non-stick baking paper followed by aluminium foil. Place the ham, top-side down, in a tight-fitting, deep-sided roasting pan. Pour the glaze over the ham and roast for 40 minutes. Remove from the oven and reduce the oven temperature to 200°C (400°F). Turn the ham over, baste with the glaze and roast for a further 20–25 minutes or until golden.

Remove the ham from the pan and place on a large serving platter. Brush the remaining glaze over the ham before carving (see *cook's tips*, page 29) to serve. **SERVES 12-14**
+ *This recipe calls for a whole leg of ham, with the bone in, that has been pre-cured and pre-cooked. If you can't buy a pre-cooked ham in your part of the world (sometimes the case in the UK), ask your local butcher for a cured leg and follow their cooking instructions before glazing.*

cheat's glazed ham

○ Before serving the ham, remove the foil and paper that covers the hock. Wrap with calico and tie with ribbon for a festive touch.

cook's tips

○ This clever glazed ham is super-simple to prepare but retains the sticky-sweet depth of flavour that defines traditional Christmas ham. There's no need for fussy scoring or studding with tiny cloves, just remove the skin and pour over the warm spiced glaze. The ham will bathe in a generous amount of the glaze while it's in the oven, eliminating the need for persistent basting and ensuring the ham stays moist.

○ When purchasing your ham, be sure to buy a cooked, cured leg.

○ It's not very often that an entire leg of ham is devoured on Christmas day. This, of course, means ham sandwiches all-round for days to follow. Ham will keep longer if it's on the bone, so only slice as much as you need and store the rest in the fridge.

○ Keep the leg of ham fresh in the fridge by covering it in a clean ham bag or tea towel that's been soaked in 2 parts water and 1 part white vinegar. Ensure the bag has been well wrung out before placing it over the ham and refrigerating. Repeat the process with the water and vinegar every 3 days. The ham should last for up to 2 weeks.

carving ham

YOU WILL NEED
a wooden chopping board
a damp tea towel
a large cook's knife

step 1

1. It helps to have some baking paper or calico fastened over the hock of the ham so you can hold it securely while you're carving. Place the chopping board on top of the tea towel to prevent it from moving. Starting at the front of the ham, slice on a slight angle down to the bone.

step 2

2. Run the knife lengthways along the bone to remove the slices. When one-third of the ham has been sliced, remove the bone, cutting it at the joint.

juniper, blackcurrant and vincotto glazed ham

juniper, blackcurrant and vincotto glazed ham

1 tablespoon juniper berries
1.5 litres apple and blackcurrant juice
2 tablespoons Dijon mustard
2 cloves garlic, crushed
1 sprig bay leaves (about 6 leaves)
1 sprig rosemary
2 cups (350g) light brown sugar
1 cup (250ml) vincotto
1 x 6–7kg ham leg (see *note*, page 26)

Place the juniper berries, juice, mustard, garlic, bay leaves, rosemary, sugar and vincotto in a medium saucepan over high heat. Bring to the boil, reduce the heat to medium and simmer for 30 minutes.

Preheat oven to 200°C (400°F). Use a sharp knife to score the skin around the sides and hock of the ham, before using your fingers to gently remove the rind. Trim any excess fat. Wrap the ham hock in non-stick baking paper then aluminium foil. Place the ham, top-side down, in a large deep-sided roasting pan. Pour the glaze over the ham and roast for 20 minutes. Turn and roast, basting every 10 minutes with the glaze, for a further 20 minutes or until the ham is golden and sticky.

Serve the ham with any remaining glaze. **SERVES 12–14**

bourbon, marmalade and ginger glazed ham

1½ cups (510g) store-bought orange marmalade
30g ginger, peeled and thinly sliced
1 clove garlic, crushed
2 cups (350g) light brown sugar
3 cups (750ml) water
2 tablespoons Dijon mustard
¼ cup (60ml) bourbon
1 x 6–7kg ham leg (see *note*, page 26)
cloves, for decorating

Place the marmalade, ginger, garlic, sugar, water and mustard in a medium saucepan over medium heat. Bring to a simmer, whisking to combine. Cook for 15 minutes or until slightly reduced. Add the bourbon, whisk to combine and remove from the heat.

Preheat oven to 180°C (350°F). Lightly grease a large wire rack over a roasting pan lined with aluminium foil. Use a sharp knife to score the skin around the sides and hock of the ham, before using your fingers to gently remove the rind. Trim any excess fat. Wrap the ham hock in non-stick baking paper then aluminium foil. Score the fat of the ham in a diamond pattern and push 1 clove into the centre of each diamond. Place the ham on the rack and pour the glaze over. Roast, brushing with the glaze every 15 minutes, for 1 hour or until the ham is golden and sticky.

Serve the ham with any remaining glaze. **SERVES 12–14**

bourbon, marmalade and ginger glazed ham

spiced pomegranate and orange glazed ham

spiced pomegranate and orange glazed ham

2 sticks cinnamon
4 star-anise
1 cup (250ml) orange juice
1½ cups (260g) light brown sugar
¼ cup (60ml) pomegranate molasses
¼ cup (90g) honey
1 x 6–7kg ham leg (see *note*, page 26)
4 oranges, peeled, thinly sliced and patted dry

Preheat oven to 180°C (350°F). Place the cinnamon, star-anise, juice, sugar, pomegranate molasses and honey in a medium saucepan over medium heat and bring to the boil, stirring to dissolve the sugar. Cook for 4–6 minutes or until syrupy.

Lightly grease a large wire rack over a roasting pan lined with aluminium foil. Use a sharp knife to score the skin around the sides and hock of the ham, before using your fingers to gently remove the rind. Trim any excess fat. Wrap the ham hock in non-stick baking paper then aluminium foil. Place the ham on the rack and brush with the glaze. Arrange the orange slices over the ham, overlapping slightly. Carefully brush with the glaze and roast the ham for 40 minutes, brushing with glaze halfway. Increase the oven temperature to 200°C (400°F). Brush the ham with the glaze and roast for a further 5 minutes or until golden and caramelised.

Serve the ham with the remaining glaze. SERVES 12–14

apple cider, mustard and sage glazed ham

3 cups (750ml) apple juice
1 litre alcoholic apple cider
1 cup (250ml) maple syrup
2 cups (350g) light brown sugar
¼ cup (70g) hot English mustard
1 cup (250ml) apple cider vinegar
10 cloves
8 bay leaves
1 bunch sage leaves (about 6 sprigs)
1 x 6–7kg ham leg (see *note*, page 26)

Place the juice, cider, maple syrup, sugar, mustard, vinegar, cloves, bay leaves and sage in a large saucepan over high heat. Bring to the boil and cook for 30 minutes or until reduced and syrupy. Strain the glaze into a large heatproof jug, discarding the solids.

Preheat oven to 200°C (400°F). Use a sharp knife to score the skin around the sides and hock of the ham, before using your fingers to gently remove the rind. Trim any excess fat. Wrap the ham hock in non-stick baking paper then aluminium foil. Place the ham, top-side down, in a deep-sided roasting pan. Pour the glaze over the ham and roast for 1 hour. Turn the ham over and roast for a further 30 minutes or until golden brown and sticky.

Serve the ham with the remaining glaze. SERVES 12–14

apple cider, mustard and sage glazed ham

season the turkey breast

brown both sides

pour in the stock

strain the poaching liquid

make a roux for the gravy

add the poaching liquid

poached turkey breast with lemon and thyme gravy

1 tablespoon extra virgin olive oil
50g unsalted butter
1 x 1.5kg turkey breast fillet, skin on
  (see *cook's tips*, page 39)
sea salt and cracked black pepper
4 eschalots (French shallots), peeled and halved
3 cups (750ml) chicken stock
10 sprigs lemon thyme
1 tablespoon finely shredded lemon rind
1 teaspoon black peppercorns
50g unsalted butter, extra
¼ cup (35g) plain (all-purpose) flour

Heat the oil and butter in a large heavy-based saucepan over medium heat. Sprinkle the turkey with salt and pepper and add to the pan, skin-side down, with the eschalots. Cook the turkey for 5 minutes each side or until golden. Add the stock, thyme, lemon rind and peppercorns and bring to a simmer. Reduce the heat to low, cover with a tight-fitting lid and poach for 30 minutes or until the turkey is cooked through.

Remove the turkey from the poaching liquid, cover with aluminium foil and set aside to keep warm. Strain the poaching liquid into a heatproof jug, discarding the solids.

Melt the extra butter in a large saucepan over high heat until bubbling. Add the flour and cook, stirring, for 2–3 minutes or until golden. Gradually pour in the poaching liquid, stirring until smooth. Cook, stirring continuously, for a further 2 minutes or until the gravy has thickened.

Place the turkey on a serving platter. Slice and serve with the gravy (see *cook's tips*, page 39). **SERVES 4–6**

poached turkey breast with
lemon and thyme gravy

○ Substitute a little of the
chicken stock for white wine
if you wish, and add a couple
of bay leaves to the poaching
liquid for extra flavour.

lemon and thyme gravy

cook's tips

∘ It goes without saying that choosing to serve a turkey breast, instead of roasting the entire bird, is an easier option. But it's also a good solution if you're short on time, are having a small simple Christmas, or wish to include turkey as part of your festive banquet menu.

∘ This recipe will serve 6–8 if part of a menu. If you wish to serve the turkey as a main, with just a couple of sides, it will serve 4–6.

∘ By poaching the turkey breast, not only will you end up with tender, succulent meat infused with the delicious flavours it was cooked in, you'll also create a tasty stock to enrich your gravy. It'll mean one less dish crowding the oven, too – the turkey can simmer on the stovetop while a glazed ham, a loin of pork or trays of vegetables are roasting below.

∘ It's important to use a good heavy-based saucepan for this recipe, and why not use the same saucepan that the turkey was poached in to make the gravy – easy!

carving turkey

YOU WILL NEED
a large wooden chopping board
a large cook's knife
a large carving fork

step 1

step 3

1. Using a large, sharp knife, cut straight down the side of the turkey to remove the legs, with drumstick and thigh as 1 piece. You may need to apply a little pressure to get through the joint.

step 2

2. Locate the breastbone, cut down the centre of the turkey and then along the side of the bone away from you to remove the whole breast, with the wing still attached.

3. Cut the leg through the joint to separate the thigh from the drumstick. Slice the breast across the grain into pieces to serve. Repeat with the other side of the turkey.
Tip: Even if you're not serving the whole turkey, it's best to carve it all at once, as meat left on the bone will often continue cooking and dry out. Leftovers will then remain juicy and they'll take up less room in the fridge.

ginger brined roast turkey with pear and potato gratin

ginger brined roast turkey with pear and potato gratin

1 cup (175g) light brown sugar
1 onion, quartered
1 head garlic, halved horizontally
2 cups (600g) rock salt
1 cup (250ml) apple cider vinegar
25g ginger, peeled and thinly sliced
5 litres water
1.25 litres dry ginger ale
1 x 5kg turkey
80g unsalted butter, softened
pear stuffing
2 tablespoons extra virgin olive oil
1 onion, finely chopped
2 cloves garlic, crushed
2 William (firm green) pears, peeled, cored and chopped
⅓ cup rosemary leaves, chopped
sea salt and cracked black pepper
¼ cup (95g) stem ginger+, chopped
1 tablespoon Dijon mustard
½ cup (80g) toasted pine nuts
4 cups (280g) sourdough breadcrumbs
1 egg
pear and potato gratin
2.5kg sebago (starchy) potatoes, peeled and thinly sliced
4 William (firm green) pears, peeled, cored and thinly sliced
½ cup (125ml) hot single (pouring) cream

Place the sugar, onion, garlic, salt, vinegar, ginger and 1 litre of the water in a large saucepan over high heat. Bring to the boil, stirring to dissolve the salt. Allow to cool slightly. Pour the brining liquid into a large (10-litre-capacity) non-reactive container++. Add the dry ginger ale and the remaining water and stir to combine. Using your hands, carefully loosen the skin from the flesh of the turkey breasts. Lower the turkey, breast-side down, into the brine. Cover and refrigerate for 6 hours (but no longer).

To make the pear stuffing, place the oil in a large non-stick frying pan over high heat. Add the onion and garlic and cook, stirring, for 4 minutes. Add the pear, rosemary, salt and pepper and cook for 2 minutes. Transfer to a large bowl and add the ginger, mustard, pine nuts, breadcrumbs and egg. Mix well to combine.

Remove the turkey from the container, discarding the brine, and pat dry with absorbent kitchen paper. Spoon the stuffing into the cavity. Using your hands, spread the butter under the skin. Tie the legs with kitchen string, tuck the wings underneath and set aside.

Preheat oven to 200°C (400°F). To make the pear and potato gratin, lightly grease a 29cm x 40cm deep-sided roasting pan. Layer the potato and pear in the base of the pan and sprinkle with salt. Pour the hot cream over the gratin.

Top the gratin with the turkey. Cover with aluminium foil and roast for 1 hour. Remove the foil, reduce the oven temperature to 180°C (350°F) and roast for a further 1 hour or until the turkey is golden and the juices run clear when tested with a skewer. Cover with aluminium foil and allow to rest for 20 minutes, before serving. SERVES 6-8

+ *Stem ginger is ginger that's been preserved in sugar syrup. It's available from specialty grocers and Asian supermarkets. If unavailable, you can use crystallised ginger instead.*
++ *Non-reactive materials include glass, plastic and stainless steel.*

prosecco brined turkey breast with brussels sprouts and speck

¼ cup (75g) rock salt
¼ cup (45g) light brown sugar
2 sprigs tarragon
2 bunches thyme (about 12 sprigs)
1 lemon, thinly sliced
1.25 litres water
3 cups (750ml) prosecco
2 x 1.5kg turkey breast fillets, skin on
1 tablespoon extra virgin olive oil
sea salt and cracked black pepper
350g speck or bacon, chopped
500g Brussels sprouts, halved
1 bunch thyme (about 6 sprigs), extra
lemon garlic butter
100g unsalted butter, softened
1 clove garlic, crushed
1 teaspoon finely grated lemon rind

Place the salt, sugar, tarragon, thyme, lemon and 2 cups (500ml) of the water in a medium saucepan over high heat. Bring to the boil and cook for 4 minutes, stirring to dissolve the salt. Allow to cool slightly. Pour the brining liquid into a large (5-litre-capacity) non-reactive container[+]. Add the prosecco and another 2 cups (500ml) of the water. Using your hands, carefully loosen the skin from the flesh of the turkey breasts. Lower the turkey, skin-side down, into the brine. Cover and refrigerate for 2 hours (but no longer).

To make the lemon garlic butter, place the butter, garlic and lemon rind in a small bowl and mix to combine.

Remove the turkey from the container, discarding the brine, and pat dry with absorbent kitchen paper. Using your hands, spread the lemon garlic butter under the skin.

Place the oil in a large heavy-based frying pan over medium heat. Sprinkle the turkey with salt and pepper. Add 1 turkey breast to the pan, skin-side down. Cook for 4 minutes each side or until golden brown. Remove from the pan and repeat with the remaining turkey. Return both turkey breasts to the pan, skin-side up. Add the remaining 1 cup (250ml) of water, cover with a tight-fitting lid and cook for 20 minutes or until golden and cooked through. Remove the turkey from the pan, loosely cover with aluminium foil and reserve the cooking liquid.

Wipe the pan out and return to medium heat. Add the speck and cook, stirring, for 4 minutes or until crispy. Remove and set aside. Increase the heat to high, add the Brussels sprouts and cook, stirring, for 1 minute or until lightly charred. Add the extra thyme and reserved liquid and cook for 2 minutes.

Serve turkey with the sprouts and crispy speck. **SERVES 4–6**
+ *Non-reactive materials include glass, plastic and stainless steel.*

prosecco brined turkey breast with brussels sprouts and speck

redcurrant glazed roast turkey with crispy tarragon

redcurrant glazed roast turkey with crispy tarragon

1 sprig bay leaves (about 6 leaves)
2 sprigs rosemary
1 cup (320g) store-bought redcurrant jelly
2 tablespoons Dijon mustard
1 cup (250ml) red wine
½ cup (125ml) maple syrup
2 cups (500ml) chicken stock
12 heads single-clove garlic+, skin on
1 x 4kg turkey, butterflied and halved++
sea salt and cracked black pepper
¼ cup (60ml) extra virgin olive oil
2 bunches tarragon (about 12 sprigs)

Preheat oven to 180°C (350°F). Place the bay leaves, rosemary, jelly, mustard, wine, maple syrup and stock in a medium saucepan over medium heat and bring to the boil, whisking until combined. Pour the glaze into a large deep-sided roasting pan and add the garlic. Add the turkey, skin-side up, and sprinkle with salt and pepper. Cover with aluminium foil and roast for 1 hour. Remove the foil and roast, brushing every 15 minutes with the pan juices, for a further 45 minutes or until the turkey is sticky, golden and the juices run clear when tested with a skewer. Carefully remove the turkey from the pan, reserving the garlic and any glaze. Loosely cover the turkey with aluminium foil and set aside to rest for 20 minutes.

Heat the oil in a medium non-stick frying pan over medium heat. Working in batches, add the tarragon and cook for 30 seconds or until crisp.

Top the turkey with the crispy tarragon, sprinkle with pepper and serve with the reserved garlic and glaze. SERVES 6-8
+ Single-clove garlic is available from greengrocers. If you can't find it, use large unpeeled garlic cloves.
++ Butterflying a turkey allows it to cook faster and more evenly. To butterfly a turkey, position the turkey, breast-side down, on a board so the back is facing up and the drumsticks are facing towards you. Using sharp kitchen scissors or chicken shears, cut closely along both sides of the backbone, remove the bone and discard. Turn the turkey breast-side up, and press down firmly on the breastbone to flatten. To halve, use a sharp knife to cut the turkey down the centre. You can ask your butcher to butterfly the turkey for you.

rolled turkey with maple and bacon stuffing

50g unsalted butter, chopped
4 rashers bacon, finely chopped
1 brown onion, finely chopped
2 cloves garlic, crushed
500g Granny Smith (green) apples, peeled, cored and grated
1 tablespoon thyme leaves, chopped
3 cups (210g) coarse fresh breadcrumbs
1 tablespoon finely grated orange rind
¼ cup (60ml) maple syrup
sea salt and cracked black pepper
1 x 1.8kg turkey breast fillet, skin on
orange and maple glaze
100g unsalted butter, chopped
½ cup (125ml) maple syrup
½ cup (125ml) orange juice
1 stick cinnamon

Place the butter in a large non-stick frying pan over high heat. Add the bacon, onion and garlic and cook, stirring, for 4–5 minutes or until lightly browned. Add the apple and thyme and cook for 4–5 minutes or until golden. Transfer to a large bowl and add the breadcrumbs, orange rind, maple syrup, salt and pepper. Mix to combine and set aside to cool completely.

To make the orange and maple glaze, place the butter, maple syrup, juice and cinnamon in a small saucepan over high heat and cook, stirring, until the butter is melted. Bring to the boil and cook for 8–10 minutes or until reduced slightly.

Preheat oven to 200°C (400°F). Lightly grease a wire rack and place over a roasting pan lined with aluminium foil. Place the turkey, skin-side down, on a board. Cut the thickest part of the breast horizontally and open out to make one even fillet. Cover with 2 layers of plastic wrap and, using a meat mallet, flatten to 1.5cm thick. Remove the plastic and arrange the stuffing down one long edge of the fillet. Sprinkle with salt and pepper and roll to enclose. Secure with kitchen string and place the turkey on the rack. Brush with the glaze and roast for 20 minutes. Brush again and roast for 10–20 minutes or until golden and cooked through. Cover with lightly greased aluminium foil and set aside to rest for 10 minutes. Place the remaining glaze in a small saucepan over high heat. Bring to the boil and cook for 1–2 minutes or until warmed through.

Slice the turkey and serve with the warm glaze. SERVES 6-8

rolled turkey with maple and bacon stuffing

classic roast turkey with lemon sage butter

classic roast turkey with lemon sage butter

1 x 4–5kg turkey[+]
2 tablespoons extra virgin olive oil
1.25 litres chicken stock
1kg baby onions, peeled
herb stuffing
50g unsalted butter, chopped
1 brown onion, thinly sliced
3 cloves garlic, thinly sliced
¼ cup thyme leaves, roughly chopped
½ cup oregano leaves, roughly chopped
sea salt and cracked black pepper
3 cups (210g) roughly torn sourdough bread
2 medium truss tomatoes, thinly sliced
1 tablespoon Dijon mustard
lemon sage butter
60g unsalted butter, softened
1 tablespoon finely grated lemon rind
¼ cup sage leaves, finely chopped
1 tablespoon Dijon mustard

To make the herb stuffing, place the butter in a large non-stick frying pan over medium heat. Add the onion and garlic and cook, stirring, for 4–5 minutes or until golden. Add the thyme, oregano, salt and pepper and cook for 1 minute. Transfer to a large bowl and add the bread. Allow to cool slightly before adding the tomato and mustard. Mix to combine and set aside.

To make the lemon sage butter, place the butter, rind, sage, mustard, salt and pepper in a small bowl and mix to combine.

Preheat oven to 180°C (350°F). Lightly grease a large wire rack over a roasting pan. Using your hands, carefully loosen the skin from the flesh of the turkey breasts and spread the lemon sage butter underneath. Spoon the stuffing into the cavity and secure with a skewer. Tie the legs with kitchen string and tuck the wings underneath. Place the turkey on the rack, brush with oil, sprinkle with salt and pepper and pour the stock into the pan. Cover with lightly greased aluminium foil and roast for 2 hours 15 minutes. Remove the foil, add the onions to the stock and roast, basting every 15 minutes with the stock, for a further 45 minutes – 1 hour or until golden and the juices run clear when tested with a skewer[+]. Cover with aluminium foil and allow to rest for 20 minutes. Serve with the roasted onions. **SERVES 6-8**
+ *Allow 18–20 minutes cooking time per 500g of stuffed turkey.*

tarragon and juniper brined roast turkey

2 cups (500g) table salt
1 cup (175g) light brown sugar
2 bulbs garlic, halved horizontally
2 tablespoons crushed fennel seeds
¼ cup (20g) juniper berries
1 tablespoon black peppercorns, crushed
2 lemons, sliced
2 bunches tarragon (about 12 sprigs)
8 bay leaves
8 litres water, plus 2½ cups (625ml) extra
1 x 5.5kg turkey
2 tablespoons extra virgin olive oil
lemon garlic butter
150g unsalted butter, chopped and softened
1 teaspoon finely grated lemon rind
2 cloves garlic, crushed

Place the salt, sugar, garlic, fennel, juniper, peppercorns, half the lemon slices, half the tarragon, the bay leaves and 1 litre of the water in a medium saucepan over high heat and bring to the boil. Cook for 10 minutes, stirring to dissolve the salt. Allow to cool slightly and pour the brining liquid into a large (10-litre-capacity) non-reactive container[+]. Add the remaining 7 litres of water and stir to combine.

Using your hands, carefully loosen the skin from the flesh of the turkey breasts. Tie the legs with kitchen string and tuck the wings underneath. Lower the turkey, breast-side down, into the brine. Cover and refrigerate for 6 hours (but no longer).

To make the lemon garlic butter, place the butter, lemon rind and garlic in a small bowl and mix to combine.

Preheat oven to 180°C (350°F). Lightly grease a large wire rack over a roasting pan. Remove the turkey from the container, discarding the brine, and pat dry with absorbent kitchen paper. Using your hands, spread the butter under the skin. Place the remaining lemon and tarragon inside the cavity. Place the turkey on the rack and brush with the oil. Pour the extra water into the pan, cover with lightly greased aluminium foil and roast for 1 hour. Uncover and roast for a further 45 minutes or until golden and the juices run clear when tested with a skewer. Cover with aluminium foil and allow to rest for 20 minutes, before serving. **SERVES 6-8**
+ *Non-reactive materials include glass, plastic and stainless steel.*

tarragon and juniper brined roast turkey

maple and prosciutto wrapped brined turkey breasts with herb butter

2 cups (500ml) dry white wine
2 cups (500ml) water
¼ cup (60g) table salt
½ cup (90g) light brown sugar
6 cloves garlic, bruised
4 sprigs flat-leaf parsley
1 bunch sage (about 6 sprigs)
4 sprigs thyme
2 bay leaves
1 litre water, extra
2 x 1.8kg turkey breast fillets, skin on
20 slices prosciutto
¼ cup (60ml) maple syrup
Dijon mustard, to serve
store-bought fruit chutney, to serve
herb butter
2 cloves garlic, crushed
⅓ cup finely chopped flat-leaf parsley
2 teaspoons finely chopped thyme
2 teaspoons finely chopped sage
2 teaspoons finely grated lemon rind
300g unsalted butter, softened
2 teaspoons sea salt flakes
2 teaspoons cracked black pepper

Place the wine, water, salt, sugar, garlic, parsley, sage, thyme and bay leaves in a medium saucepan over high heat. Bring to the boil, stirring to dissolve the salt. Allow to cool slightly and pour the brining liquid into a large (6-litre-capacity) non-reactive container[+]. Add the extra water and stir to combine. Using your hands, carefully loosen the skin from the flesh of the turkey breasts. Lower the turkey breasts, skin-side down, into the brine. Cover and refrigerate for 2–3 hours (but no longer).

To make the herb butter, place the garlic, parsley, thyme, sage, lemon rind, butter, salt and pepper in a medium bowl. Mix well to combine and set aside.

Preheat oven to 180°C (350°F). Line a large baking tray with aluminium foil. Remove the turkey from the container, discarding the brine, and pat dry with absorbent kitchen paper. Spread the herb butter under the skin. Lay 10 slices of the prosciutto on a board, overlapping slightly. Top with a turkey breast, skin-side down. Wrap the prosciutto around the turkey breast, pressing to secure. Repeat with the remaining prosciutto and turkey. Place the turkey breasts on the tray and roast for 1 hour or until golden and the juices run clear when tested with a skewer. Brush the prosciutto with the maple syrup, loosely cover with aluminium foil and allow to rest for 15 minutes.

Thinly slice the turkey and serve with mustard and fruit chutney. SERVES 6–8
+ *Non-reactive materials include glass, plastic and stainless steel.*

maple and prosciutto wrapped brined turkey breasts with herb butter

vincotto roasted chicken with herb and sherry stuffing

vincotto roasted chicken with herb and sherry stuffing

1 x 1.8kg chicken
¼ cup (60ml) vincotto
2 bunches (600g) sweet black seedless grapes,
    cut into small bunches
tarragon butter
¼ cup finely chopped tarragon leaves
100g unsalted butter, softened
sea salt and cracked black pepper
herb and sherry stuffing
50g unsalted butter
2 eschalots (French shallots), finely chopped
2 tablespoons thyme leaves
1 tablespoon finely chopped rosemary leaves
½ cup (125ml) dry sherry
3 cups (210g) fresh sourdough breadcrumbs

To make the tarragon butter, place the tarragon, butter, salt and pepper in a small bowl and mix until smooth. Set aside.

To make the herb and sherry stuffing, melt the butter in a large non-stick frying pan over medium heat. Add the eschalot, thyme, rosemary, salt and pepper and cook, stirring, for 3–4 minutes, or until soft. Add the sherry and cook for 1–2 minutes or until syrupy. Remove from the heat, add the breadcrumbs and mix to combine.

Preheat oven to 180°C (350°F). Lightly grease a large heavy-based baking dish. Using your hands, carefully loosen the skin from the flesh of the chicken breasts and push the tarragon butter underneath. Fill the cavity of the chicken with the stuffing and tie the legs with kitchen string to secure. Place the chicken in the dish. Brush with 1 tablespoon of the vincotto and sprinkle with salt and pepper. Roast for 40 minutes. Add the grapes to the dish and drizzle with the remaining 2 tablespoons of vincotto. Roast for a further 30 minutes or until the chicken is golden and cooked through and the grapes are soft.

Sprinkle the chicken with pepper to serve. SERVES 6–8
Tip: You can stuff and butter the chicken up to 2 days in advance. Keep refrigerated and brush with the vincotto just before roasting.

bacon wrapped spatchcocks with fig and herb stuffing

4 x 500g spatchcocks (baby chickens)
¾ cup (240g) store-bought fruit chutney,
    plus extra to serve
20 slices streaky bacon
6 x 3cm-thick slices brioche loaf
¼ cup (60ml) extra virgin olive oil
1 bunch sage (about 6 sprigs)
fig and herb stuffing
1 tablespoon extra virgin olive oil
1 onion, finely chopped
2 cloves garlic, crushed
¼ cup (50g) dried figs, chopped
1 tablespoon dried currants
2 tablespoons sweetened dried cranberries, chopped
2 tablespoons red wine vinegar
½ cup flat-leaf parsley leaves, finely chopped
¼ cup sage leaves, finely chopped
2 teaspoons Dijon mustard
2½ cups (450g) torn brioche loaf
sea salt and cracked black pepper

Preheat oven to 180°C (350°F). To make the fig and herb stuffing, place the oil in a large non-stick frying pan over medium heat. Add the onion, garlic, figs, currants and cranberries and cook, stirring, for 4 minutes or until softened. Add the vinegar and cook for 2 minutes. Transfer to a large bowl. Add the parsley, sage, mustard, torn brioche, salt and pepper and mix well to combine.

Spoon the stuffing into the cavity of each spatchcock and tie the legs with kitchen string. Brush 1 tablespoon of the chutney over each spatchcock. Wrap each spatchcock in bacon. Place the brioche slices in a large, deep-sided roasting pan and spread with the remaining chutney. Top with the spatchcocks and roast for 30 minutes or until golden and cooked through.

While the spatchcocks are roasting, heat the oil in a small non-stick frying pan over high heat. Working in batches, cook the sage for 30 seconds or until crisp.

Sprinkle the spatchcocks with pepper and serve with the crispy sage and extra chutney. SERVES 4

bacon wrapped spatchcocks with fig and herb stuffing

port and pistachio stuffed chicken with quince glaze

port and pistachio stuffed chicken with quince glaze

1 x 1.7kg chicken
2 tablespoons extra virgin olive oil
port and pistachio stuffing
100g unsalted butter
1 brown onion, finely chopped
2 cloves garlic, crushed
⅓ cup (80ml) port
3 cups (210g) fresh sourdough breadcrumbs
1 teaspoon finely grated orange rind
1 tablespoon thyme leaves, finely chopped
½ cup (70g) shelled pistachios, roughly chopped
⅓ cup (50g) dried cherries[+]
sea salt and cracked black pepper
quince glaze
1¼ cups (300g) store-bought quince jelly
1 tablespoon malt vinegar

Preheat oven to 180°C (350°F). To make the port and pistachio stuffing, melt the butter in a medium non-stick frying pan over medium heat. Add the onion and garlic and cook, stirring, for 6 minutes or until soft. Add the port and cook for a further 2 minutes. Transfer to a large bowl and add the breadcrumbs, orange rind, thyme, pistachios, cherries, salt and pepper. Mix well to combine.

Line a baking tray with non-stick baking paper. Fill the cavity of the chicken with the stuffing. Place on the tray and tie the legs with kitchen string. Rub the skin with oil and sprinkle with salt. Roast for 1 hour or until golden and cooked through.

To make the quince glaze, place the jelly and vinegar in a small saucepan over low heat. Cook, stirring, for 3–4 minutes or until syrupy.

Brush the chicken with the glaze, placing any extra in a jug, to serve. SERVES 4

+ *You can use sweetened dried cranberries in place of the cherries.*

spice rubbed roast duck with cherry sauce

1 x 2.3kg duck
4 cloves
1 teaspoon fennel seeds
½ teaspoon cumin seeds
1 teaspoon ground allspice
1 teaspoon light brown sugar
2 teaspoons sea salt flakes
1 small orange, quartered
1½ cups (330g) caster (superfine) sugar
¼ cup (60ml) Campari
2½ cups (375g) frozen pitted cherries
3 sticks cinnamon
4 star-anise
4 strips orange peel
25g ginger, peeled and thinly sliced

Lightly grease a large wire rack over a deep-sided roasting pan. Using a skewer, pierce the skin of the duck all over. Place the duck in a heatproof bowl, cover with boiling water and allow to stand for 30 seconds. Drain, place on the rack and pat dry with absorbent kitchen paper.

Place the cloves, fennel and cumin seeds in a mortar and pound with a pestle until fine. Add the allspice, brown sugar and salt and mix to combine. Rub the spice mixture all over the duck. Place the orange quarters in the cavity and fasten with a metal skewer. Refrigerate, uncovered, for 1 hour or until the skin is dry.

Preheat oven to 180°C (350°F). Roast the duck for 45 minutes. Remove the pan from the oven and carefully set the duck aside on the rack. Drain any excess fat from the pan juices. Add the caster sugar, Campari, cherries, cinnamon, star-anise, orange peel and ginger to the pan and mix to combine. Return the rack with the duck to sit over the pan and roast for a further 1 hour or until the cherry sauce is sticky and reduced and the duck is golden.

Serve the duck with the cherry sauce. SERVES 4-6

spice rubbed roast duck with cherry sauce

score the pork rind

sprinkle with salt

rub the salt in well

spoon the stuffing inside

spread evenly to coat

roll up and tie to secure

roasted pork loin with sour cherry stuffing

1 x 3kg boneless pork loin, trimmed
⅓ cup (40g) sea salt flakes
2 tablespoons extra virgin olive oil
sour cherry stuffing
1 tablespoon extra virgin olive oil
1 small brown onion, finely chopped
2 cloves garlic, crushed
2 tablespoons thyme leaves
3 cups (210g) fresh sourdough breadcrumbs
1 egg
1 tablespoon Dijon mustard
¼ cup (35g) shelled unsalted pistachios, chopped
⅓ cup (90g) sour cherry relish (see *recipe*, page 61),
    plus extra to serve⁺
sea salt and cracked black pepper

Score the pork rind at 1cm intervals. Sprinkle the rind with
2 tablespoons of the salt and rub in to coat. Refrigerate
the pork, uncovered, for 2–3 hours (see *cook's tips*, page 61).

While the pork is resting, make the sour cherry stuffing.
Heat the oil in a medium non-stick frying pan over medium
heat. Add the onion, garlic and thyme and cook, stirring, for
5–6 minutes or until just golden. Transfer the mixture to a
large bowl and add the breadcrumbs, egg, mustard, pistachios,
relish, salt and pepper. Mix well to combine and set aside.

Preheat oven to 220°C (425°F). Lightly grease a wire rack
over a roasting pan lined with non-stick baking paper. Brush
the salt from the pork and pat with absorbent kitchen paper
to remove any excess moisture. Turn the pork, rind-side down,
and spread evenly with the stuffing. Roll to enclose and secure
with kitchen string. Brush the rind with the oil and rub with the
remaining 2 tablespoons of salt, pushing it into the incisions.
Place the pork on the rack and roast for 25 minutes. Reduce
the oven temperature to 200°C (400°F) and roast for a
further 30–40 minutes or until cooked to your liking. Cover
with aluminium foil and allow to rest for 15 minutes.

Remove the foil and kitchen string and place the pork on
a serving platter. Slice and serve with extra relish. SERVES 6–8
⁺ *You can use store-bought cranberry sauce instead of the
sour cherry relish, if you prefer.*

roasted pork loin with sour cherry stuffing

sour cherry relish

sour cherry relish

1 tablespoon extra virgin olive oil
1 small brown onion, finely chopped
1 tablespoon thyme leaves
500g frozen pitted sour cherries
1 tablespoon finely grated orange rind
¼ cup (60ml) orange liqueur
⅓ cup (80ml) red wine vinegar
1 cup (220g) caster (superfine) sugar
sea salt and cracked black pepper

Place the oil in a medium saucepan over medium heat. Add
the onion and thyme and cook for 1–2 minutes or until just
golden. Add the cherries, orange rind, liqueur, vinegar, sugar,
salt and pepper and stir to combine. Bring to the boil and cook
for 30–35 minutes or until reduced and glossy. Allow to cool
completely at room temperature. **MAKES 2 CUPS**
*Tip: This relish will keep refrigerated in an airtight container
for up to 2 weeks. Bring to room temperature before serving.*

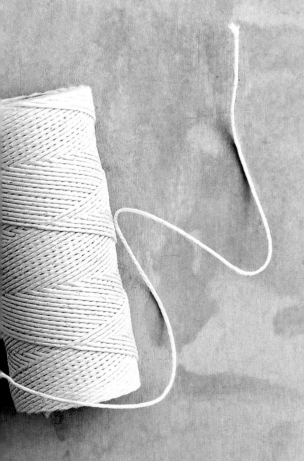

cook's tips

○ Salty, crunchy crackling
is arguably the most
sought-after part of roast
pork. There are a few simple
tricks to making sure it's
extra-crispy every time.
Drying out the rind of the
pork, before roasting, is
important. If time permits,
the day before you roast the
pork, place it, uncovered,
on a wire rack over a tray
in the fridge. Leave it
overnight, then dry it with
absorbent kitchen paper.

○ Scoring the rind exposes
more surface area to heat,
making it crisper, faster.

○ Rubbing the skin with oil
and salt adds loads of crunch
to the crackling.

○ Make sure your oven is
nice and hot. Preheat it to
220°C (425°F) and roast the
pork for 25 minutes before
reducing the temperature
for the remaining time.

○ The sour cherry relish can
be used in a similar way to
cranberry sauce. Its tart,
fruity flavour is perfect
with the pork, but it's also
great with ham or turkey.

score the pork rind   rub with sea salt flakes

drizzle and rub in the oil

crispy pork belly with fennel salt

2 tablespoons sea salt flakes
1 x 2kg piece boneless pork belly, rind scored at 1cm intervals
1 tablespoon vegetable oil
peach, chilli and rosemary chutney, to serve (see *recipe*, below)
fennel salt
2 teaspoons fennel seeds, toasted and crushed
2 tablespoons black sea salt flakes

Preheat oven to 180°C (350°F). Rub half the salt into the pork rind. Drizzle with the oil and rub to coat. Place the pork, rind-side down, in a roasting pan and roast for 1 hour. Increase the oven temperature to 200°C (400°F). Turn the pork, sprinkle the rind with the remaining salt and roast for a further 1 hour or until the rind is golden and crunchy.

To make the fennel salt, place the fennel and black salt in a small bowl and mix to combine.

Slice the pork and place on a serving platter. Sprinkle with the fennel salt and serve with chutney. **SERVES 8–10**

peach, chilli and rosemary chutney

6 peaches, cut into wedges
1 white onion, finely chopped
2 cloves garlic, crushed
½ teaspoon dried chilli flakes
2 sprigs rosemary
1 cup (250ml) apple cider vinegar
1½ cups (330g) caster (superfine) sugar
1 teaspoon sea salt flakes

Place the peach, onion, garlic, chilli, rosemary, vinegar, sugar and salt in a large saucepan over high heat. Bring to the boil, reduce the heat to medium and cook, stirring occasionally, for 40–45 minutes or until thickened[+]. Remove the rosemary sprigs and pour into sterilised jars[++]. Allow to cool. **MAKES 5 CUPS**
+ *To test whether the chutney is ready, chill a small saucer in the freezer. Place a spoonful of chutney on the cold saucer and run your finger through the middle. If the line remains, it's done.*
++ *To sterilise glass jars, preheat oven to 120°C (250°F). Wash the jars and their (metal) lids in soapy water, rinse and place on an oven tray. Heat for 20 minutes. Allow to cool before filling.*
Tip: This chutney will keep refrigerated for up to 3 weeks.

crispy pork belly with fennel salt
peach, chilli and rosemary chutney

crispy pork belly with spiced plum sauce

crispy pork belly with spiced plum sauce

1 tablespoon extra virgin olive oil
2 tablespoons sea salt flakes
1 x 2kg piece boneless pork belly, rind scored at 1cm intervals
spiced plum sauce
½ cup (90g) light brown sugar
½ cup (125ml) red wine vinegar
4 whole dried chillies
2 star-anise
1 stick cinnamon
400g ripe plums, halved

Preheat oven to 180°C (350°F). Rub the oil and salt into the pork rind. Place the pork, rind-side down, on a baking tray and roast for 1 hour. Increase the oven temperature to 200°C (400°F), turn the pork and roast for a further 1 hour 20 minutes or until the skin is golden and crunchy.

While the pork is roasting, make the spiced plum sauce. Place the sugar, vinegar, chillies, star-anise and cinnamon in a medium non-stick frying pan over high heat and bring to a simmer. Add the plums and cook, turning occasionally, for 8–10 minutes or until just soft and the sauce has reduced.

Serve the pork with the spiced plum sauce. **SERVES 6**

pork belly with garlic, caramelised onion and quince sauce

300g store-bought quince paste, roughly chopped
½ cup (175g) golden syrup
3 cups (750ml) water
1 cup (250ml) malt vinegar
3 brown onions, thickly sliced
1 x 2.5kg piece boneless pork belly
10 heads single-clove garlic+, skin on
1 bunch thyme (about 6 sprigs)

Preheat oven to 180°C (350°F). Place the quince paste, golden syrup, water and vinegar in a medium saucepan over high heat. Bring to the boil and cook, whisking, for 1 minute or until smooth.

Place the onion in a large, deep-sided roasting pan and top with the pork, rind-side down. Add the garlic and thyme and pour the quince mixture over the top. Cover tightly with aluminium foil and roast for 3 hours 30 minutes. Turn the pork and roast, uncovered, for a further 30 minutes or until tender.

Slice the pork and serve with the garlic, caramelised onion and quince sauce. **SERVES 6-8**
+ *Single-clove garlic is available from greengrocers. If you can't find it, use large garlic cloves.*

pork belly with garlic, caramelised onion and quince sauce

fennel roasted pork leg with baby figs and pickled onions

fennel roasted pork leg with baby figs and pickled onions

1 x 4.5kg pork leg, rind scored at 2cm intervals
1 tablespoon extra virgin olive oil
1 teaspoon caraway seeds
1 teaspoon fennel seeds
⅓ cup (40g) sea salt flakes
2 x 400g jars marinated baby figs in syrup+
2 x 440g jars pickled onions, drained
2 sticks cinnamon
1 cup (250ml) water
store-bought horseradish cream, to serve

Preheat oven to 220°C (425°F). Line a large deep-sided roasting pan with non-stick baking paper. Place the pork, rind-side up, in the pan and rub with the oil. Wrap the hock with non-stick baking paper then aluminium foil and set aside.

Place the caraway and fennel seeds in a mortar and pound with a pestle until coarsely ground. Add the salt and mix to combine. Rub the spice mixture into the pork rind and set aside at room temperature for 30 minutes.

Roast the pork for 30 minutes. Reduce the oven temperature to 180°C (350°F) and roast for a further 1 hour 30 minutes.

Carefully remove the pork from the pan. Discard the pan juices and paper. Add the figs and their syrup, the onions, cinnamon and water. Mix to combine and place the pork on top. Increase the oven temperature to 220°C (425°F). Roast for 30 minutes or until the rind is crisp and the pork is tender.

Serve pork with the figs, onions and horseradish. SERVES 8–10
+ Marinated baby figs are available from delicatessens and online.

malt vinegar and bourbon sticky pork belly

1 cup (250ml) bourbon whiskey
1½ cups (375ml) malt vinegar
2 cups (500ml) water
3 cups (525g) dark brown sugar
10 cloves garlic, bruised and peeled
1 cup (350g) golden syrup
2 sticks cinnamon
4 bay leaves
1 x 2.5kg piece boneless pork belly
cracked black pepper, for sprinkling

Preheat oven to 180°C (350°F). Place the bourbon, 1 cup (250ml) of the vinegar, the water, sugar, garlic, golden syrup, cinnamon and bay leaves in a medium saucepan over high heat and bring to the boil. Cook, stirring occasionally, for 2–3 minutes or until thickened slightly.

Place the pork, rind-side down, to fit snugly in a deep-sided roasting pan. Pour the sauce over the pork, cover tightly with aluminium foil and roast for 3 hours 30 minutes. Turn the pork, add the remaining ½ cup (125ml) of vinegar and cover with the foil. Roast for a further 30 minutes or until tender. Remove the pork from the pan and skim the fat from the surface of the sauce. Strain the sauce into a heatproof jug.

Slice the pork and top with the sauce. Sprinkle with pepper to serve. SERVES 6–8

malt vinegar and bourbon sticky pork belly

remove from the freezer

halve the lobster

prep the butter mixture

spread it over the flesh

grilled lobster with taramasalata butter

1kg rock salt
4 x 600g green (raw) lobsters, cleaned and halved
   (see *cook's tip*, below)
taramasalata butter
250g unsalted butter, chopped and softened
1 cup (260g) store-bought taramasalata
sea salt and cracked black pepper

To make the taramasalata butter, place the butter, taramasalata, salt and pepper in a medium bowl. Mix to combine and set aside.
   Preheat oven grill (broiler) to high. Divide the rock salt between 2 large oven trays and spread evenly. Place the lobster halves, shell-side down, on the salt and spread the flesh with half the butter mixture. Cook the lobster, in batches, for 6–8 minutes or until the butter is golden and the lobster is just cooked. Top with the remaining taramasalata butter and sprinkle with pepper to serve. **SERVES 8**
Tip: You can make the taramasalata butter up to 2–3 days in advance and keep it refrigerated.

cook's tip

∘ To prepare live lobsters, place them in a clean tea towel and wrap to enclose. Freeze for 1 hour to sedate them. Remove and place 1 lobster, shell-side up, on a large chopping board. Using a large sharp knife, halve the head section, pressing the knife firmly from the neck down towards the eyes. Rotate the board and halve the body section, now cutting down towards the tail. Clean the insides, using a spoon to scrape them out. Pat the flesh dry with absorbent kitchen paper. Repeat with the remaining lobsters.

grilled lobster with taramasalata butter

portuguese-style barbecued seafood platter

portuguese-style barbecued seafood platter

1½ tablespoons smoked paprika
3 teaspoons sweet paprika
1½ teaspoons dried chilli flakes
3 cloves garlic, crushed
1 tablespoon finely grated lemon rind
¾ cup (180ml) extra virgin olive oil
¼ cup (60ml) red wine vinegar
2 x 375g raw blue swimmer crabs
4 scallops on the half shell
6 green (raw) king prawns (shrimp), shells intact
    and halved lengthways
4 sardines, filleted
6 small squid tubes, cleaned
500g mussels, cleaned
sea salt and cracked black pepper
lemon wedges and aioli (optional), to serve

Preheat a large chargrill pan or barbecue over high heat.
Place the smoked and sweet paprika, the chilli, garlic, lemon
rind, oil and vinegar in a small bowl and mix to combine.
Reserve and set aside ¼ cup (60ml) of the dressing.

Place the crabs, scallops, prawns, sardines, squid and mussels
in a large roasting pan. Drizzle with the paprika dressing and
toss to coat.

Add the crabs to the grill and cook, covered[1], for 5 minutes
each side. Set aside and keep warm. Add the scallops, shell-side
down, and cook, covered, for 3 minutes. Set aside and keep
warm. Add the prawns, sardines and squid and cook for
1–2 minutes each side or until charred and just cooked. Set
aside and keep warm. Add the mussels and cook, covered,
for 1–2 minutes or until opened.

Place the seafood onto a large serving platter. Sprinkle
with salt and pepper and drizzle with the reserved dressing.
Serve with lemon wedges and aioli, if you like. SERVES 2
+ If using a barbecue, close the lid to cover. If using a chargrill
pan, cover with a tight-fitting lid or a large metal bowl.

beetroot and juniper glazed salmon with horseradish mash

1 x 800g side sashimi-grade salmon, skin on
4 large beetroot (1kg), trimmed and chopped
3 cups (750ml) apple juice
6 cloves garlic
1 teaspoon finely grated lemon rind
2 tablespoons juniper berries
1 tablespoon each sea salt flakes and black peppercorns
1 bunch tarragon (about 6 sprigs)
½ cup (90g) light brown sugar
1 tablespoon apple cider vinegar
2 tablespoons extra virgin olive oil
horseradish mash
1kg sebago (starchy) potatoes, peeled and chopped
1 cup (250ml) single (pouring) cream
2 tablespoons freshly grated horseradish[+]
sea salt and cracked black pepper

Place the salmon to fit snugly in a deep-sided baking dish. Place
the beetroot, juice, garlic, lemon rind, juniper, salt, pepper
and half the tarragon in a blender and blend until smooth.
Pour the mixture over the salmon, ensuring the salmon is
submerged. Cover with plastic wrap and refrigerate for 3 hours.

Preheat oven to 240°C (475°F). Line a large baking tray
with non-stick baking paper. Remove the salmon from the
dish, wipe off any excess marinade and set aside, skin-side
down, on the tray. Reserve ½ cup (125ml) of the beetroot
mixture and strain into a small saucepan. Place over medium
heat. Add the sugar and vinegar, stir to combine and bring
to the boil. Cook for 10 minutes or until syrupy.

Roast the salmon, brushing every 10 minutes with the
beetroot glaze, for 30 minutes or until dark golden.

To make the horseradish mash, place the potato in a medium
saucepan of cold, salted water over high heat. Bring to the boil
and cook for 8 minutes or until tender. Drain and return to the
pan. Add the cream, horseradish and salt and mash until smooth.

Heat the oil in a small non-stick frying pan over high heat.
Add the remaining tarragon and cook for 30 seconds or until
crisp. Serve the salmon with the horseradish mash, remaining
glaze, salt, pepper and the crispy tarragon. SERVES 4
+ If you can't find fresh horseradish, you can substitute with
grated horseradish (available in a jar from the supermarket).

beetroot and juniper glazed salmon with horseradish mash

rosemary salt baked whole snapper

rosemary salt baked whole snapper

2 cups rosemary leaves
6 cloves garlic
1kg rock salt
2 eggwhites
8 long thick sprigs rosemary, extra
1 x 1.2kg whole snapper, cleaned
1 lemon, sliced

Preheat oven to 220°C (425°F). Place the rosemary leaves, garlic and ⅓ cup (100g) of the salt in a food processor and process until finely chopped. Transfer to a large bowl and add the remaining 3 cups (900g) of salt. Add the eggwhites and mix to combine.

Place half the salt mixture in the base of a large baking dish. Top with the extra rosemary sprigs and the snapper. Place the lemon in the cavity of the fish. Pour the remaining salt mixture onto the fish and gently press to seal. Roast for 25 minutes or until cooked to your liking.

Allow to cool slightly before carefully removing the salt crust to serve. SERVES 4

Tips: Baking a whole fish in a salt crust not only looks impressive, it keeps moisture in and intensifies flavour, resulting in fine taste and texture. Brush away any extra salt, using a pastry brush, before serving.

steamed snapper with coriander and cucumber salad

2 x 450g whole baby snapper, cleaned
1 lime, thinly sliced
2 long red chillies, thinly sliced
50g ginger, peeled and finely shredded
½ cup micro (baby) coriander (cilantro) leaves (optional)
coriander and cucumber salad
2 tablespoons rice wine vinegar
2 teaspoons sesame oil
1 clove garlic, crushed
½ cup coriander (cilantro) leaves, finely chopped
1 long red chilli, seeded and finely chopped
1 tablespoon tamari+
5 cucumbers (650g), sliced diagonally

Rinse the fish and pat dry with absorbent kitchen paper. Score the flesh, 3cm apart, on each side. Place lime, chilli and ginger into the cavity of each fish.

Line a 36cm bamboo steamer with non-stick baking paper. Add the fish to the steamer, cover with a tight-fitting lid and place over a wok or large deep-sided frying pan of boiling water. Steam for 12 minutes or until the fish is just cooked.

To make the coriander and cucumber salad, place the vinegar, oil, garlic, coriander, chilli and tamari in a medium jug and whisk to combine. Place the cucumber in a medium bowl, add half the dressing and toss to combine.

Place the fish on a serving platter and sprinkle with the micro coriander leaves. Serve with the salad and remaining dressing. SERVES 4

+ Tamari is a Japanese style of soy sauce. It's traditionally made with little to no wheat, so is often gluten-free (however, be sure to check the label if you have gluten intolerances). Find tamari in most supermarkets. If unavailable, use regular or light soy sauce.

steamed snapper with coriander and cucumber salad

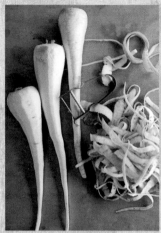

peel the parsnips

sprinkle them with sugar

thyme and champagne roasted parsnips

2kg parsnips, peeled, quartered and cut into 8cm lengths
½ cup (90g) light brown sugar
16 sprigs lemon thyme, plus extra to serve
2 cups (500ml) Champagne or sparkling wine
sea salt and cracked black pepper

Preheat oven to 220°C (425°F). Divide the parsnip between
2 large roasting pans. Sprinkle with the sugar and toss to
combine. Divide the thyme and Champagne between the
pans, toss to coat and sprinkle with salt and pepper. Roast,
turning halfway, for 30–35 minutes or until the parsnip is
golden and caramelised.

Transfer the parsnip to a serving plate, top with extra
thyme and sprinkle with salt and pepper to serve. **SERVES 6-8**

toss to combine

top with the thyme sprigs

pour in the champagne

thyme and champagne roasted parsnips

broccoli with lemon butter and thyme breadcrumbs

broccoli with lemon butter and thyme breadcrumbs

1.5kg broccoli, cut into florets
100g unsalted butter, chopped
1 tablespoon lemon rind
1 tablespoon lemon juice
¼ cup (60ml) dry white wine
sea salt and cracked black pepper
½ cup (35g) fresh sourdough breadcrumbs
¼ cup lemon thyme leaves
1 tablespoon extra virgin olive oil

Preheat oven to 200°C (400°F). Place the broccoli in a large heatproof bowl and cover with boiling water. Allow to stand for 2 minutes, drain well and place in a large roasting pan.

Place the butter, lemon rind, lemon juice and wine in a small saucepan over medium heat and stir until the butter is melted. Pour the sauce over the broccoli and sprinkle with salt and pepper.

Place the breadcrumbs, thyme and oil in a medium bowl and mix to combine. Sprinkle the breadcrumb mixture over the broccoli and roast for 20 minutes or until golden and the broccoli is tender. SERVES 6

amaretti, prosciutto and herb stuffed apples

1 tablespoon extra virgin olive oil
1 onion, finely chopped
2 cloves garlic, thinly sliced
sea salt and cracked black pepper
6 slices prosciutto, chopped
2 cups (160g) fruit sourdough breadcrumbs
8 amaretti biscuits (30g), crushed
1 cup flat-leaf parsley leaves, chopped
¼ cup marjoram leaves
1 egg
2 tablespoons sherry vinegar
12 x Royal Gala (red) apples

Preheat oven to 180°C (350°F). Place the oil in a large non-stick frying pan over high heat. Add the onion, garlic, salt and pepper and cook, stirring, for 4–5 minutes or until golden. Transfer to a large bowl. Add the prosciutto, breadcrumbs, amaretti, parsley, marjoram, egg and vinegar and mix to combine.

Line a large baking tray with non-stick baking paper. Slice the tops from the apples and set aside. Using a teaspoon, scoop out the cores and discard, leaving the bases of the apples intact. Fill the cavities of the apples with the breadcrumb mixture and place on the tray. Return the tops to the apples and bake for 35–40 minutes or until golden brown and softened.

Allow the apples to cool slightly before serving. MAKES 12

amaretti, prosciutto and herb stuffed apples

honey and almond hasselback pumpkin

honey and almond hasselback pumpkin

1 x 1.8kg butternut pumpkin (squash), halved lengthways,
    peeled and seeds removed
1 tablespoon extra virgin olive oil
½ cup (180g) honey
2 tablespoons malt vinegar
14 bay leaves
½ cup (80g) almonds, toasted and chopped
sea salt and cracked black pepper

Preheat oven to 220°C (425°F). Line a large baking tray with
non-stick baking paper. Place half the pumpkin, cut-side down,
on a chopping board. Place a chopstick, lengthways, on each
side of the pumpkin. Using a very sharp knife, carefully slice
through the pumpkin to the chopsticks at 5mm intervals.
Repeat with the remaining pumpkin half.
    Place the pumpkin on the tray, cut-side down, and drizzle with
the oil. Cover tightly with aluminium foil and roast for 1 hour.
Uncover and roast for a further 20 minutes or until golden.
    Place the honey, vinegar and bay leaves in a small saucepan
over high heat. Bring to the boil and cook for 4–5 minutes
or until slightly reduced. Spoon half the honey glaze over the
pumpkin and place the bay leaves in the incisions. Roast the
pumpkin for a further 5–10 minutes or until tender and golden.
    Sprinkle with the almonds, salt and pepper and drizzle with
the remaining honey glaze to serve. **SERVES 6**

whole roasted cauliflower in white wine and garlic butter

1.5kg cauliflower, trimmed with leaves intact
2 cups (500ml) dry white wine
1 cup (250ml) vegetable or chicken stock
100g unsalted butter, chopped
2 tablespoons Dijon mustard
1 bunch thyme (about 6 sprigs)
8 cloves garlic, skin on
4 strips lemon rind
sea salt and cracked black pepper

Preheat oven to 220°C (425°F). Place the cauliflower,
wine, stock, butter, mustard, thyme, garlic, lemon rind,
salt and pepper in a deep-sided roasting pan. Cover tightly
with aluminium foil and roast, basting with the pan juices
every 30 minutes, for 1 hour 30 minutes or until tender.
    Uncover, baste with the pan juices and roast for a
further 15 minutes or until golden brown to serve. **SERVES 6**

whole roasted cauliflower in white wine and garlic butter

potato and herb bread wreath

1kg rock salt
1.5kg sebago (starchy) potatoes
1½ cups (375ml) milk
75g unsalted butter, chopped
1½ tablespoons caster (superfine) sugar
3 teaspoons dry yeast
4½ cups (675g) plain (all-purpose) flour
½ teaspoon sea salt flakes
3 eggs
3 cups flat-leaf parsley leaves, finely chopped
¼ cup rosemary leaves, finely chopped
¼ cup thyme leaves
⅓ cup (80ml) extra virgin olive oil

Preheat oven to 220°C (425°F). Place the rock salt on a baking tray and top with the potatoes. Prick the potatoes all over with a metal skewer and roast for 1 hour or until soft. Allow to cool slightly. Cut the potatoes in half and scoop the flesh into a medium bowl, discarding the skins, and set aside.

While the potato is cooling, place half the milk in a small saucepan over high heat and bring to just below the boil. Remove from the heat, add the butter and sugar and stir until the butter is melted. Add the yeast and the remaining milk and stir to combine. Set aside in a warm place for 5 minutes or until the surface is foamy.

Place the flour, sea salt, eggs and the yeast mixture in the bowl of an electric mixer fitted with a dough hook and beat for 5 minutes or until the dough is smooth and elastic. Place the dough in a lightly oiled bowl, cover with plastic wrap and set aside in a warm place for 30 minutes or until doubled in size.

Sprinkle the dough with the potato and gently knead to combine. Divide the dough into roughly 34 x 1-tablespoon portions and roll into balls.

Line a 24cm round cake tin with non-stick baking paper, allowing 3cm of the paper to sit above the edge. Lightly grease an 8cm-tall x 8cm-wide ovenproof ramekin[+] and position it in the centre of the tin. Place the parsley, rosemary, thyme and oil in a small bowl and mix to combine. Roll the dough balls in the herb mixture and place in the tin. Cover with plastic wrap and set aside in a warm place for 30 minutes or until risen.

Preheat oven to 180°C (350°F). Bake the bread for 25 minutes or until golden brown and cooked through. While still warm, remove the ramekin and allow the bread to cool in the tin for 5 minutes, before turning out and serving. **SERVES 8-10**
+ *It's important the ramekin is at least 8cm tall, as the dough will continue to rise as it bakes.*
Tips: A sprig or two of fresh bay leaves or rosemary, pushed into the baked bread, makes a lovely addition to the wreath. Place it in the centre of the table for easy sharing and it will double as a festive centrepiece.

potato and herb bread wreath

duck fat potato and onion galette

duck fat potato and onion galette

1.2kg sebago (starchy) potatoes, peeled and thinly sliced
  using a mandolin
¼ cup (60g) duck fat, melted[+]
sea salt and cracked black pepper
2 onions, thinly sliced into rounds

Preheat oven to 200°C (400°F). Line an 18cm ovenproof frying pan with non-stick baking paper. Place the potato, duck fat, salt and pepper in a large bowl and gently toss to combine. Arrange one-third of the potato in the base of the pan, overlapping the slices. Top with half the onion. Repeat with half the remaining potato and all the remaining onion. Finish with a layer of potato.

Bake for 45 minutes or until the potato is tender and golden. Carefully transfer to a serving plate and sprinkle with salt and pepper to serve. SERVES 6
+ You can buy duck fat in jars or tins at delicatessens, specialty grocers and at most supermarkets.

chestnut, bacon and sage stuffing rolls

50g unsalted butter
2 small brown onions, finely chopped
2 cloves garlic, crushed
100g rindless bacon, finely chopped
⅓ cup (80ml) dry sherry, plus 1 tablespoon extra
8 soft fresh dates (160g), pitted and chopped
1 x 240g can cooked chestnuts[+], chopped
¼ cup (35g) slivered almonds, toasted and chopped
3 cups (210g) fresh breadcrumbs
¼ cup each finely chopped sage and flat-leaf parsley leaves
1 teaspoon finely grated lemon rind
2 eggs, lightly beaten
1 teaspoon each sea salt flakes and cracked black pepper
24 thin slices streaky bacon[++]
2 tablespoons honey

Preheat oven to 180°C (350°F). Melt the butter in a large non-stick frying pan over medium heat. Add the onion, garlic and bacon and cook, stirring, for 5–6 minutes or until soft. Add the sherry and dates and cook, stirring, for 1 minute. Transfer to a large bowl and add the chestnuts, almonds, breadcrumbs, sage, parsley, lemon rind, egg, salt and pepper. Mix to combine and set aside.

Cut 2 large pieces of aluminium foil and 2 large pieces of non-stick baking paper. Lay 1 piece of foil on a flat surface and top with 1 sheet of baking paper. Arrange 12 of the bacon slices, overlapping slightly, on the paper. Place half the stuffing along one edge of the bacon and shape into a log. Using the foil and paper to help you, roll the bacon to enclose the stuffing, wrapping to secure. Repeat with the remaining foil, baking paper, bacon and stuffing. Place the rolls on a baking tray and roast for 20 minutes.

Place the extra sherry and honey in a small bowl and mix to combine. Remove the rolls from the foil and paper and return to the tray. Brush with the honey glaze and roast for a further 20 minutes or until crisp. Slice to serve. SERVES 8–10
+ Buy canned chestnuts from grocers and specialty food shops.
++ Ask your butcher to thinly slice streaky bacon for you, or use flat pancetta slices.
Tip: These rolls can be assembled 2 days ahead and refrigerated. If you want to serve them alongside pork or turkey, simply add them to the same oven in the last 40 minutes of roasting time.

chestnut, bacon and sage stuffing rolls

crispy leaf potatoes with oregano salt

crispy leaf potatoes with oregano salt

5.5kg large sebago (starchy) potatoes, peeled
1¼ cups (310g) duck fat⁺, melted
1 tablespoon sea salt flakes
1 teaspoon cracked black pepper
oregano salt
¼ cup oregano leaves
2 tablespoons sea salt flakes

Preheat oven to 200°C (400°F). Trim the rounded edges of each potato to make large rectangles and thinly slice on a mandolin. Place in a large bowl, add the duck fat, salt and pepper and toss to combine.

Working along the short edge of a 24cm x 37cm roasting pan, arrange the potato upright from right to left to fill the pan. Roast for 1 hour 15 minutes or until golden and crisp.

To make the oregano salt, place the oregano and half the salt in a small food processor and process until finely chopped. Transfer to a small bowl, add the remaining salt and mix to combine.

Sprinkle the potatoes with oregano salt to serve. **SERVES 8-10**
+ *You can buy duck fat in jars or tins at delicatessens, specialty grocers and at most supermarkets.*

glazed root vegetable tarte tatin

2 medium carrots (240g), peeled
2 medium parsnips (500g), peeled
2 small sweet potatoes (kumara) (350g), peeled
2 turnips (450g), peeled
¼ cup (60ml) extra virgin olive oil
sea salt and cracked black pepper
⅓ cup (80ml) water
1 cup (220g) caster (superfine) sugar
1 tablespoon red wine vinegar
100g stracchino⁺, sliced
4 sheets frozen butter puff pastry, thawed
1 bunch lemon thyme (about 6 sprigs), to serve

Preheat oven to 220°C (425°F). Slice the carrots, parsnips, sweet potatoes and turnips into 1cm-thick rounds. Divide between 2 oven trays, drizzle with the oil and sprinkle with salt and pepper. Toss to combine and roast, turning halfway, for 30 minutes or until golden and tender.

While the vegetables are roasting, place the water and sugar in a medium saucepan over medium heat and cook, stirring, until the sugar has dissolved. Increase the heat to high and cook, without stirring, for 6–8 minutes or until light caramel in colour. Remove from the heat and carefully add the vinegar, stirring to combine. Working quickly, pour the caramel evenly onto a 24cm x 37cm roasting pan⁺⁺. Arrange the vegetables on top of the caramel, overlapping if necessary, and top with the cheese. Place the 4 sheets of pastry over the top of the vegetables (pastry will overlap) allowing 2cm to overhang around the edge of the pan. Gently press the overlapping pastry to seal and tuck in the overhanging edges.

Reduce the oven temperature to 200°C (400°F). Place the tart on an oven tray to catch any spills and bake for 20 minutes. Reduce the oven temperature to 180°C (350°F) and bake for a further 20 minutes or until the pastry is puffed and golden. Allow to stand in the pan for 5 minutes before inverting onto a board.

Top with the thyme and cut into squares to serve. **SERVES 8-10**
+ *Stracchino is a young Italian cow's milk cheese. Find it in delicatessens and cheese stores. Use taleggio if unavailable.*
++ *Use a metal spoon to spread the caramel over the base of the pan. Don't worry if it doesn't spread all the way to the corners – it will spread as it bakes.*

glazed root vegetable tarte tatin

cauliflower, caramelised onion and fontina gratin

cauliflower, caramelised onion and fontina gratin

1.5kg cauliflower, trimmed and cut into florets
½ cup (140g) store-bought caramelised onion relish
1⅔ cups (410ml) single (pouring) cream
2½ cups (250g) grated fontina or gruyère
sea salt and cracked black pepper
2 tablespoons extra virgin olive oil
12 small sage leaves
finely grated parmesan, to serve

Preheat oven to 180°C (350°F). Line 2 x 30cm round baking dishes with non-stick baking paper. Cut the cauliflower florets into 1cm-thick slices and arrange them in the dishes, placing 1-teaspoon portions of caramelised onion relish between the overlapping slices. Drizzle with the cream and top with the fontina, salt and pepper. Bake for 30 minutes or until the cauliflower is just tender and the cheese is golden.

While the gratin is baking, heat the oil in a small non-stick frying pan over medium heat. Cook the sage leaves, in batches, for 30 seconds or until crisp.

Top the gratin with the crispy sage leaves and parmesan to serve. SERVES 8–10

roasted pear and rosemary brioche toasts

1 cup (175g) light brown sugar
¼ cup (60ml) apple cider vinegar
50g unsalted butter, melted
7 small corella (rosy pink) pears, quartered
1 x 400g brioche loaf
2 tablespoons rosemary leaves
1 teaspoon cracked black pepper

Preheat oven to 220°C (425°F). Line a deep-sided roasting pan with non-stick baking paper. Place the sugar, vinegar and butter in a large bowl and mix to combine. Reserve and set aside ¼ cup (60ml) of the mixture. Add the pears to the bowl with the sugar mixture and toss to coat. Transfer to the pan and roast, turning halfway, for 15 minutes or until just golden.

Line a 24cm x 37cm baking tray with non-stick baking paper. Slice the brioche loaf into 13 x 2cm-thick slices. Trim the crusts and cut each slice in half. Arrange the brioche to fit snugly on the tray. Top each rectangle with a wedge of roasted pear and pour over any pan juices. Brush each pear with the reserved sugar mixture and sprinkle with the rosemary. Bake for 15 minutes or until the brioche is toasted and the pears are golden.

Brush the pears with any remaining sugar mixture and sprinkle with the pepper to serve. SERVES 8–10
Tips: You can roast the pears 1 day in advance and keep them refrigerated in their cooking juices. Assemble the toasts the next day and bake as instructed. These toasts are perfect served alongside ham and roasted pork.

roasted pear and rosemary brioche toasts

parsnip, sweet potato and thyme yorkshire puddings

parsnip, sweet potato and thyme yorkshire puddings

1 cup (150g) plain (all-purpose) flour
4 eggs
2 teaspoons sea salt flakes
1 teaspoon cracked black pepper
1⅓ cups (330ml) milk
2 teaspoons thyme leaves
½ cup (60g) shaved parsnip⁺
1 cup (120g) shaved sweet potato (kumara)⁺
⅓ cup (80g) ghee (clarified butter), melted

Preheat oven to 220°C (425°F). Place the flour, eggs, salt, pepper, milk and thyme in a blender and blend until smooth. Allow to stand for 20 minutes. Place the parsnip and sweet potato in a small bowl and toss to combine.

Divide the ghee between 12 x ½-cup-capacity (125ml) muffin tins. Heat in the oven for 12–15 minutes or until the ghee is just smoking. Remove from the oven and, working quickly, pour ¼-cup (60ml) portions of the batter into each tin. Top with the shaved vegetables. Bake for 20–25 minutes or until puffed and golden. Allow to cool in the tins for 5 minutes before turning out to serve. MAKES 12
+ *You'll need to buy 1 parsnip and 1 sweet potato for this recipe. Use a vegetable peeler or a mandolin to shave the required amount.*

prosciutto wrapped baby carrots

1kg mixed heirloom baby carrots, trimmed and peeled
8 slices prosciutto, cut into 8cm-long strips
4 bay leaves
8 strips orange rind
2 tablespoons extra virgin olive oil
2 tablespoons maple syrup
sea salt and cracked black pepper

Preheat oven to 180°C (350°F). Lightly grease 2 large baking dishes. Wrap each carrot in a strip of prosciutto. Divide the wrapped carrots, the bay leaves and orange rind between the dishes. Drizzle with the oil and maple syrup and sprinkle with salt and pepper. Roast for 15–18 minutes or until the prosciutto is golden brown and the carrots are tender.

Sprinkle the carrots with extra pepper to serve. SERVES 6-8

prosciutto wrapped baby carrots

caramelised onion and potato stacks

2 tablespoons extra virgin olive oil
4 brown onions, trimmed and sliced into 16 thick rounds
500g sebago (starchy) potatoes, peeled and thinly sliced
⅔ cup (160ml) chicken stock
80g unsalted butter, melted
8 sprigs thyme
sea salt and cracked black pepper

Preheat oven to 180°C (350°F). Line 8 x ½-cup capacity (125ml) muffin tins with non-stick baking paper. Heat the oil in a large non-stick frying pan over medium heat. Add the onion slices and cook in batches, turning, for 3 minutes or until golden.

Place 1 onion slice in the base of each tin. Divide the potato slices between the tins and top with the remaining onion.

Divide the stock and butter between the tins and top each with a thyme sprig. Cover with aluminium foil and roast for 30 minutes. Uncover and roast for a further 30 minutes or until cooked through and golden.

Remove the stacks from the tins and sprinkle with salt and pepper to serve. MAKES 8

asparagus and feta salad

⅓ cup (80ml) lemon-flavoured extra virgin olive oil
2 tablespoons white balsamic or white wine vinegar
1 tablespoon finely chopped dill sprigs
1 tablespoon finely chopped tarragon leaves
1 tablespoon finely chopped chives
1 clove garlic, crushed
sea salt and cracked black pepper
800g asparagus, trimmed[+]
400g feta, sliced

Place the oil, vinegar, dill, tarragon, chives, garlic, salt and pepper in a small bowl and mix to combine.

Place the asparagus in a large saucepan of salted boiling water and cook for 1 minute or until just tender. Drain and refresh under cold running water. Arrange on a serving plate. Top with the feta and drizzle with dressing to serve. SERVES 8
+ To trim asparagus, either remove the woody end by bending the stalk at the base until it snaps, or shave off the tough outer skin using a vegetable peeler. Cut with a knife to make a neat edge.

greens with sage butter

700g green beans, trimmed
4 x 175g bunches broccolini (tenderstem), trimmed
150g unsalted butter, chopped
1 bunch sage (about 6 sprigs), leaves picked
sea salt and cracked black pepper

Place the beans and broccolini in a large saucepan of
salted boiling water and cook for 2 minutes or until tender.
Drain, refresh under cold running water and set aside.

Melt the butter in a large non-stick frying pan over
medium heat. Add the sage and cook for 3–4 minutes
or until crispy. Add the beans, broccolini, salt and pepper
and toss until warmed through.

Arrange the greens on a serving plate and spoon the
sage butter over to serve. SERVES 8

roast potatoes with green beans and speck

1.5kg kipfler (waxy) potatoes, halved lengthways
300g speck[+], chopped
2 tablespoons extra virgin olive oil
300g green beans, trimmed and blanched
mustard dressing
¼ cup (60ml) extra virgin olive oil
1 tablespoon white wine vinegar
1 tablespoon lemon juice
1 tablespoon Dijon mustard
sea salt and cracked black pepper

Preheat oven to 180°C (350°F). Place the potato, speck and
oil in a roasting pan, sprinkle with salt and toss to coat. Roast,
turning occasionally, for 40 minutes or until golden.

To make the mustard dressing, place the oil, vinegar, lemon
juice, mustard, salt and pepper in a bowl and whisk to combine.

Add the beans to the potatoes. Top with the dressing and
toss to combine. Transfer to a serving platter to serve. SERVES 8
+ Speck is a slab of cured ham available from delicatessens.
If unavailable, you can use bacon or flat pancetta instead.

brussels sprout, broad bean and almond salad

2 tablespoons extra virgin olive oil
80g unsalted butter
2 cloves garlic, crushed
750g Brussels sprouts, sliced
1 cup (120g) frozen peas, thawed
1 cup (140g) broad (fava) beans, peeled and blanched
sea salt and cracked black pepper
⅓ cup (45g) slivered almonds
⅓ cup sage leaves
1 tablespoon finely grated lemon rind

Heat half the oil and the butter in a large non-stick frying pan over high heat. Add the garlic and Brussels sprout and cook, stirring occasionally, for 2–3 minutes or until golden. Add the peas and broad beans and cook for a further 1–2 minutes. Sprinkle with salt and pepper, transfer to a serving plate and keep warm.

Add the remaining oil, the almonds and sage to the pan and cook, stirring, for 1 minute or until golden. Add the lemon rind, toss to combine and spoon onto the greens to serve. SERVES 4–6

potato, apple and horseradish mash

1.5kg sebago (starchy) potatoes, peeled and roughly chopped
6 Granny Smith (green) apples, peeled, cored and chopped
40g unsalted butter
1½ tablespoons grated fresh horseradish[+]
sea salt and cracked black pepper
⅓ cup (80g) crème fraîche

Place the potato in a large saucepan of cold, salted water. Bring to the boil and cook for 15 minutes. Add the apple and cook for a further 8 minutes or until the potato and apple are tender. Drain well, return to the pan and mash until smooth. Add the butter, horseradish and salt and mix to combine.

Place the mash in a serving bowl and top with the crème fraîche. Sprinkle with pepper to serve. SERVES 4–6
+ *Fresh horseradish is available from greengrocers and lends this mash excellent flavour. If unavailable, use horseradish cream.*

zucchini salad with honey lemon dressing

300g zucchini (courgette), thinly sliced using a mandolin
400g yellow squash, thinly sliced using a mandolin
2 cups mint leaves
½ cup (40g) shaved ricotta salata+ or parmesan
sea salt and cracked black pepper
honey lemon dressing
¼ cup (60ml) extra virgin olive oil
2 tablespoons lemon juice
2 teaspoons honey

To make the honey lemon dressing, place the oil, lemon juice and honey in a small jug and whisk to combine.

   Place the zucchini, squash, mint and ricotta salata on a serving plate. Drizzle with the honey lemon dressing and sprinkle with salt and pepper to serve. **SERVES 4–6**
+ *Ricotta salata is a hard, salted ricotta that has been aged and dried. Find it at delicatessens and Italian grocery stores.*
Tip: If you don't have a mandolin, you can use a peeler to thinly slice the vegetables.

baked parsnip, sweet potato and gruyère mash

750g sweet potatoes (kumara), peeled and chopped
750g parsnips, peeled and chopped
30g unsalted butter
¼ cup (60g) sour cream
1 cup (125g) finely grated gruyère
sea salt and cracked black pepper
2 eggs
1½ cups (100g) fresh brioche or sourdough breadcrumbs
1 clove garlic, crushed
1 tablespoon extra virgin olive oil
2 tablespoons thyme or lemon thyme leaves

Preheat oven to 180°C (350°F). Place the potato and parsnip in a large saucepan of boiling water and cook for 10–15 minutes or until tender. Drain and return to the pan. Add the butter, sour cream, gruyère, salt and pepper and mash until smooth. Add the eggs, 1 at a time, and mix well. Spoon into a 1.5-litre-capacity baking dish. Place the breadcrumbs, garlic and oil in a small bowl and mix to combine. Sprinkle onto the mash and bake for 10 minutes or until golden. Top with thyme to serve. **SERVES 4–6**

dill, rosemary and yoghurt biscuits

dill, rosemary and yoghurt biscuits

1¾ cups (245g) wholemeal (whole-wheat) spelt flour
½ cup (140g) natural Greek-style (thick) yoghurt
1 cup (125g) finely grated firm goat's cheese
1 teaspoon sea salt flakes
½ teaspoon cracked black pepper
50g unsalted butter, softened
¼ cup dill sprigs, finely chopped
¼ cup rosemary leaves, finely chopped

Place the flour, yoghurt, cheese, salt, pepper and butter in a food processor and process until the mixture comes together. Add the dill and rosemary and pulse until just combined.

Turn the dough out and bring together to form a ball. Roll out between 2 sheets of non-stick baking paper to 4mm thick. Refrigerate for 30 minutes.

Preheat oven to 180°C (350°F). Line 2 large baking trays with non-stick baking paper. Using a 7cm round cookie cutter, cut 28 rounds from the dough, re-rolling as necessary. Place on the trays. Bake for 15 minutes or until firm and golden. Allow to cool on the trays or transfer to wire racks before serving. MAKES 28

basil lavosh

1 teaspoon dry yeast
½ cup (125ml) lukewarm water
1 teaspoon caster (superfine) sugar
2 cups (300g) 00 flour⁺, plus extra for dusting
1 teaspoon sea salt flakes, plus extra for sprinkling
¼ cup (60ml) extra virgin olive oil, plus extra for brushing
1 eggwhite
2 cups basil leaves

Place the yeast, water and sugar in a small bowl and mix to combine. Set aside in a warm place for 5–10 minutes or until the surface is foamy.

Place the flour and salt in a large bowl and mix to combine. Make a well in the centre and add the oil and the yeast mixture. Mix until a dough forms. Turn the dough out and knead for 5–6 minutes or until smooth and elastic. Place in a large lightly oiled bowl, cover with plastic wrap and set aside in a warm place for 20 minutes or until risen slightly.

Preheat oven to 180°C (350°F). Line 2 large baking trays with non-stick baking paper. Divide the dough into 8 pieces and roll each piece out on a lightly floured surface to make a 1mm-thick oval shape. Lightly brush each lavosh with eggwhite and top with the basil leaves, pressing to secure. Place 2 lavosh on each tray, brush with extra oil and sprinkle with extra salt. Bake for 12 minutes or until puffed and golden brown. Transfer to wire racks and repeat with the remaining lavosh, extra oil and salt. Allow to cool before serving. MAKES 8

+ 00 flour is a superfine baker's flour that makes for soft, stretchy dough. It's available from the baking aisle of most supermarkets.

basil lavosh

burnt butter, honey and sage crackers

burnt butter, honey and sage crackers

1¼ cups (200g) wholemeal (whole-wheat) plain
    (all-purpose) flour
1½ cups (135g) rolled oats
½ cup (40g) finely grated parmesan
1 teaspoon sea salt flakes
1 egg
200g unsalted butter, chopped
¼ cup (90g) honey
1 bunch sage (about 6 sprigs), leaves picked
1 eggwhite, extra

Place the flour, oats, parmesan, salt and egg in a food
processor and process until the oats are finely chopped.
    Place the butter, honey and half the sage in a small
non-stick frying pan over high heat. Cook for 2–3 minutes
or until the butter starts to foam. Remove from the heat and
allow to cool slightly. Remove and discard the sage and add
the butter mixture to the food processor. Process until the
mixture just comes together. Turn the dough out and bring
together to form a ball. Roll out between 2 sheets of non-stick
baking paper to make a 4mm-thick 30cm x 40cm rectangle.
    Pick the remaining sage leaves from the stalks. Remove
the top sheet of paper from the dough. Lightly brush the
dough with eggwhite and top with the sage leaves, pressing
gently to secure. Return the paper to the dough and gently
roll over it to secure the leaves. Remove and discard the top
sheet of paper, cut the dough into squares and prick each
with a fork. Using the paper to help you, slide the dough
onto a large baking tray and refrigerate for 30 minutes.
    Preheat oven to 160°C (325°F). Bake the crackers for
20 minutes or until golden and crisp. Allow to cool on the
tray before breaking into squares to serve. MAKES 30

mixed olive and thyme biscotti

3 cups (450g) plain (all-purpose) flour
2 teaspoons baking powder
1½ cups (200g) pitted mixed olives+, sliced
½ teaspoon sea salt flakes
2 tablespoons thyme leaves, finely chopped
1 cup (80g) finely grated pecorino
2 eggs
½ cup (125ml) milk

Preheat oven to 160°C (325°F). Line a 20cm square slice tin
with non-stick baking paper. Place the flour, baking powder,
olives, salt, thyme and pecorino in a large bowl and mix to
combine. Make a well in the centre, add the eggs and milk
and mix well to combine. Press the mixture into the base of
the tin. Bake for 30 minutes or until golden. Remove from
the tin and set aside to cool slightly.
    Line 3 large baking trays with non-stick baking paper.
Using a serrated knife, slice the dough into 2mm-thick
pieces and place on the trays. Bake for 20 minutes or until
crisp and golden. Transfer to wire racks to cool completely
before serving. MAKES 40
+ Try a mix of Kalamata and Sicilian olives, or use your
favourite combination.

mixed olive and thyme biscotti

currant, juniper and blue cheese biscuits + parmesan, fennel and lemon thyme biscuits
basic parmesan biscuits + three-cheese biscuits + parmesan and pink peppercorn biscuits

basic parmesan biscuits

1 cup (150g) plain (all-purpose) flour
1 cup (80g) finely grated parmesan
½ cup (45g) rolled oats
100g cold unsalted butter, chopped
½ teaspoon sea salt flakes
1 egg yolk
1½ tablespoons iced water

Place the flour, parmesan, oats, butter and salt in a food processor and pulse until the mixture resembles fine breadcrumbs. Add the egg yolk and water and process until the mixture comes together. Turn the dough out and bring together to form a ball. Roll out between 2 sheets of non-stick baking paper to 5mm thick. Refrigerate for 30 minutes.

Preheat oven to 180°C (350°F). Line 2 large baking trays with non-stick baking paper. Using a 6cm round cookie cutter, cut 20 rounds from the dough, re-rolling as necessary. Place on the trays and bake for 12–15 minutes or until golden and crisp. Allow to cool on the trays for 5 minutes. Transfer to wire racks to cool completely before serving. MAKES 20

currant, juniper and blue cheese biscuits

1 x quantity basic parmesan biscuit dough (see *recipe*, above)
1 tablespoon juniper berries
50g firm blue cheese, crumbled
¼ cup (40g) dried currants

Follow the basic parmesan biscuit dough recipe, adding the juniper berries with the parmesan. Once the mixture comes together in the food processor, add the blue cheese and currants and pulse until just combined. Roll the dough out and refrigerate as directed.

Preheat oven to 180°C (350°F). Line 2 large baking trays with non-stick baking paper. Using an 8cm round cookie cutter, cut 16 rounds from the dough, re-rolling as necessary. Place on the trays and bake for 12–15 minutes or until golden and crisp. Allow to cool on the trays for 5 minutes. Transfer to wire racks to cool completely before serving. MAKES 16

parmesan, fennel and lemon thyme biscuits

1 x quantity basic parmesan biscuit dough (see *recipe*, left)
2 teaspoons fennel seeds
2 tablespoons lemon thyme leaves

Follow the basic parmesan biscuit dough recipe, adding the fennel seeds and thyme with the egg yolk. Roll the dough out and refrigerate as directed.

Preheat oven to 180°C (350°F). Line 2 large baking trays with non-stick baking paper. Using a 7.5cm round cookie cutter, cut 16 rounds from the dough, re-rolling as necessary. Place on the trays and bake for 12–15 minutes or until golden and crisp. Allow to cool on the trays for 5 minutes. Transfer to wire racks to cool completely before serving. MAKES 16

three cheese biscuits

1 x quantity basic parmesan biscuit dough (see *recipe*, left)
⅓ cup (40g) finely grated cheddar
⅔ cup (80g) finely grated gruyère
1 tablespoon iced water, extra
½ cup (40g) finely grated parmesan, extra

Follow the basic parmesan biscuit dough recipe, adding the cheddar and half the gruyère with the oats. Add the extra iced water with the egg yolk. Roll the dough out and refrigerate as directed.

Preheat oven to 180°C (350°F). Line 3 large baking trays with non-stick baking paper. Using a 5cm round cookie cutter, cut 30 rounds from the dough, re-rolling as necessary. Place on the trays and sprinkle with the remaining gruyère and extra parmesan. Bake for 12–15 minutes or until golden and crisp. Allow to cool on the trays for 5 minutes. Transfer to wire racks to cool completely before serving. MAKES 30

parmesan and pink peppercorn biscuits

2 teaspoons pink peppercorns
1 x quantity basic parmesan biscuit dough
  (see *recipe*, page 111)
2 teaspoons cracked black pepper

Place the pink peppercorns in a mortar and grind with a pestle until finely crushed. Follow the basic parmesan biscuit dough recipe. After rolling out the dough, remove the top sheet of paper and sprinkle with both the peppers. Return the paper to the dough and gently roll again to secure. Refrigerate for 30 minutes.

Preheat oven to 180°C (350°F). Line 2 large baking trays with non-stick baking paper. Using a 6cm round cookie cutter, cut 20 rounds from the dough, re-rolling as necessary. Place on the trays and bake for 12–15 minutes or until golden and crisp. Allow to cool on the trays for 5 minutes. Transfer to wire racks to cool completely before serving. MAKES 20

wholemeal poppy seed lavosh

1 teaspoon dry yeast
⅔ cup (160ml) lukewarm water
1 teaspoon caster (superfine) sugar
1½ cups (240g) wholemeal (whole-wheat) plain
  (all-purpose) flour
2 tablespoons poppy seeds
1 teaspoon sea salt flakes, plus extra for sprinkling
¼ cup (60ml) extra virgin olive oil, plus extra for brushing

Place the yeast, water and sugar in a small bowl and mix to combine. Set aside in a warm place for 5–10 minutes or until the surface is foamy.

Place the flour, poppy seeds and salt in a large bowl and mix to combine. Make a well in the centre and add the oil and the yeast mixture. Mix until a dough forms. Turn the dough out and knead for 5–6 minutes or until smooth and elastic. Place in a large lightly oiled bowl, cover with plastic wrap and set aside in a warm place for 20 minutes or until risen slightly.

Preheat oven to 180°C (350°F). Line 2 large baking trays with non-stick baking paper. Roll the dough out on a lightly floured surface to 1mm thick. Using both 6.5cm and 7.5cm leaf-shaped cutters, cut 40 leaves from the dough. Place half the leaves on the trays. Brush with extra oil, sprinkle with extra salt and bake for 10–12 minutes or until puffed and golden brown. Transfer to wire racks and repeat with the remaining shapes, extra oil and salt. Allow to cool before serving. MAKES 40

wholemeal poppy seed lavosh

treats

Whimsical puffs of meringue, sugar-spun caramels, soft gingerbread and shimmering trifle – it must be Christmas! I do love the special kind of magic that comes with this time of year, and for me, nothing captures it quite like baking treats. Be they show-stopping desserts, charming gifts or edible decorations, I think festive sweets bring everyone joy, young and old. All my favourite recipes are here – I'll guide you through the classics, like brandy-soaked fruit cake and cloth-wrapped pudding, to more modern pavlova and trifle ideas, to cookies that are fit for a certain midnight visitor.

pour in the brandy

add the dry ingredients

add the butter mixture

mix well to combine

spread evenly in the tin

christmas cake

3 cups (450g) raisins

1½ cups (240g) sultanas

1 cup (160g) dried currants

8 soft fresh dates (160g), pitted and chopped

1 cup (140g) slivered almonds

¾ cup (180ml) brandy$^+$

250g unsalted butter, softened

1¼ cups (220g) light brown sugar

4 eggs

2¼ cups (335g) plain (all-purpose) flour, sifted

¼ teaspoon bicarbonate of (baking) soda

1½ teaspoons ground cinnamon

1 teaspoon ground allspice

2–3 tablespoons brandy$^+$, extra

Place the raisins, sultanas, currants, dates and almonds in a large bowl. Add the brandy, mix to combine and cover with plastic wrap. Allow to soak in a cool dark place overnight, mixing occasionally.

Preheat oven to 140°C (275°F). Line a 20cm square cake tin with 2 layers of non-stick baking paper. Place the butter and sugar in the bowl of an electric mixer and beat on medium speed for 8 minutes or until pale and creamy. Add the eggs, 1 at a time, beating well after each addition. Set aside.

Add the flour, bicarbonate of soda, cinnamon and allspice to the soaked fruit and mix well, ensuring the fruit is evenly coated with flour. Add the butter mixture and stir until well combined. Spoon into the tin and smooth the top. Bake for 2 hours or until cooked when tested with a skewer.

Spoon over the extra brandy while the cake is still warm. Allow to cool completely in the tin, before turning out onto a cake stand or plate to serve. SERVES 16–24

+ *While brandy is the traditional partner for fruit cake, you could also try using a dessert sherry such as Pedro Ximénez. It's an intensely sweet, dark sherry made from the Spanish grape variety of the same name. Perfect in festive cakes, puddings and custards, you can find it in liquor stores.*

Tip: Keep this cake in an airtight container in a cool, dark place for up to 2 months.

christmas cake

cook's tips

∘ The Christmas cake does benefit from long soaking of the fruit. You could macerate the fruit for 24 hours or even longer, if time permits, for a richer flavour.

∘ You can use your favourite variety of brandy, sweet sherry or rum to soak the fruit and top the cake.

∘ Double-lining the cake tin with non-stick baking paper ensures the cake doesn't become too dark during its long time in the oven.

∘ The extra brandy should be spooned over the cake while it's still warm, as the cake will soak up more liquid as it cools.

∘ You can make this cake up to 4 weeks in advance.

snowy christmas fruit cake

1 x quantity Christmas cake mixture (see *recipe*, page 116)
gingerbread snowmen (see *recipe*, page 218) and twigs,
  for decorating
icing (confectioner's) sugar, for dusting
icing
2 cups (320g) icing (confectioner's) sugar, sifted
1–1½ tablespoons boiling water

Preheat oven to 140°C (275°F). Line a 20cm round tin (10cm deep) with 2 layers of non-stick baking paper. Spoon the cake mixture into the tin. Bake for 2 hours or until cooked when tested with a skewer. Spoon over the extra brandy while the cake is still warm. Allow to cool completely in the tin.
　To make the icing, place the sugar and water in a medium bowl and mix to combine.
　Turn the cake out onto a cake stand or plate. Spoon on the icing and smooth with a palette knife. Dust the snowmen with sugar and place on the cake. Add the twigs to serve. SERVES 16–24

cranberry and fig bundt cakes with gingerbread antlers

cranberry and fig bundt cakes with gingerbread antlers

¾ cup (100g) sweetened dried cranberries
¾ cup (110g) raisins
½ cup (80g) dried currants
¾ cup (150g) dried figs, chopped
½ cup (40g) flaked almonds
½ cup (125ml) brandy, plus 2 tablespoons extra
150g unsalted butter, softened
¾ cup (135g) light brown sugar
2 eggs
1¼ cups (185g) plain (all-purpose) flour, sifted
¼ teaspoon bicarbonate of (baking) soda, sifted
1 teaspoon mixed spice
¼ cup (60ml) milk
6 gingerbread antlers, for decorating (see *recipe*, page 218)
icing (confectioner's) sugar, for dusting
24 sprigs lemon thyme, for decorating

Place the cranberries, raisins, currants, figs, almonds and brandy in a medium saucepan over medium heat. Cook, stirring occasionally, for 8 minutes or until the fruit is plump and the brandy has been absorbed. Allow to cool completely.

Preheat oven to 140°C (275°F). Grease 6 x 1-cup-capacity (250ml) mini bundt tins. Place the butter and sugar in the bowl of an electric mixer and beat for 6–8 minutes or until pale and creamy. Add the eggs, 1 at a time, beating well after each addition. Place the fruit mixture, flour, bicarbonate of soda and mixed spice in a large bowl and mix well to combine, coating the fruit in the flour. Add the butter mixture and the milk and mix to combine. Divide between the tins and place on a large oven tray. Bake for 30 minutes or until cooked when tested with a skewer. Allow to cool in the tins for 5 minutes before turning out onto a wire rack. Drizzle with the extra brandy and allow to cool completely.

Place onto cake stands or plates and top with the antlers. Dust with icing sugar and decorate with thyme to serve. **MAKES 6**

spiced sticky date, caramel and star-anise cakes

20 soft fresh dates (400g), pitted and chopped
1½ cups (375ml) boiling water
1½ teaspoons bicarbonate of (baking) soda
150g unsalted butter, chopped
1 cup (175g) light brown sugar
3 eggs
1½ cups (225g) self-raising (self-rising) flour
2 teaspoons ground cinnamon
2 teaspoons mixed spice
1⅓ cups (400g) store-bought thick caramel or dulce de leche
star-anise, for decorating

Preheat oven to 160°C (325°F). Line 2 x 12cm round cake tins with non-stick baking paper, allowing 2cm of paper to sit above the edges. Place the dates, water and bicarbonate of soda in a medium heatproof bowl and allow to soak for 10 minutes.

Place the date mixture, butter and sugar in a food processor and process until well combined. Add the eggs, flour, cinnamon and mixed spice and process until just combined. Divide the mixture between the tins. Bake for 55 minutes – 1 hour or until cooked when tested with a skewer. Allow to cool in the tins for 10 minutes before turning out onto a wire rack to cool completely.

Trim the tops from the cakes, using a large serrated knife. Place each cake onto a cake stand or plate. Using a small palette knife, spread the caramel evenly over the top and sides of the cakes. Decorate with star-anise[+]. **SERVES 6-8**
+ *The star-anise in this recipe are simply for decoration – you can remove them from the cakes before eating.*

spiced sticky date, caramel and star-anise cakes

rum and raisin brownie christmas trees

rum and raisin brownie christmas trees

1½ cups (225g) raisins
¾ cup (180ml) dark rum
200g dark chocolate, chopped
250g unsalted butter, chopped
1¾ cups (310g) light brown sugar
4 eggs
1⅓ cups (200g) plain (all-purpose) flour
¼ teaspoon baking powder
⅓ cup (35g) cocoa powder
cinnamon sticks and star-anise, for decorating
icing
1 cup (160g) icing (confectioner's) sugar, sifted
2–3 teaspoons boiling water

Preheat oven to 180°C (350°F). Line a 24cm x 34cm slice tin with non-stick baking paper. Place the raisins and rum in a small saucepan over medium heat. Cook, stirring occasionally, for 8–10 minutes or until the liquid has been absorbed. Mash roughly with a fork and set aside.

Place the chocolate and butter in a medium saucepan over low heat and stir until melted and smooth. Remove from the heat and place in a large bowl. Add the sugar, eggs, flour, baking powder and cocoa and whisk well to combine. Add the raisin mixture and mix to combine. Pour into the tin and bake for 20–22 minutes or until cooked when tested with a skewer. Allow to cool completely in the tin. Turn out and, using a 9cm tree-shaped cutter, cut 10 trees from the brownie.

To make the icing, place the sugar and water in a small bowl and mix to combine.

Spoon the icing into a piping bag fitted with a small round nozzle and pipe the icing onto the trees. Decorate with the cinnamon and star-anise to serve[+]. **MAKES 10**
+ *Remove the cinnamon sticks and star-anise before eating.*

butterscotch, peach and ginger individual panettones

2¾ teaspoons dry yeast
⅓ cup (80ml) lukewarm milk
3 cups (450g) plain (all-purpose) flour
¼ cup (55g) caster (superfine) sugar
1½ cups (240g) mixed dried peach, apricot, pear and apple[+], finely chopped
½ cup (110g) crystallised ginger, finely chopped
½ cup (125ml) butterscotch schnapps
2 teaspoons vanilla extract
4 eggs
275g unsalted butter, chopped and softened

Place the yeast and milk in a medium bowl and mix to combine. Set aside in a warm place for 5 minutes or until creamy. Add ½ cup (75g) of the flour and 1 tablespoon of the sugar and mix well to combine. Cover with plastic wrap and set aside in a warm place for 1 hour or until the mixture is foamy.

Place the mixed fruit, ginger, schnapps and vanilla in a small saucepan over high heat. Cook, stirring occasionally, for 6–7 minutes or until the schnapps is absorbed. Set aside to cool completely.

Place the eggs, yeast mixture, the remaining 2 tablespoons of sugar and the remaining 2½ cups (375g) of flour in the bowl of an electric mixer fitted with a dough hook and mix to combine. With the motor running, gradually add the butter, 1 tablespoon at a time, beating well after each addition. Add the fruit mixture and beat for 1 minute or until well combined. Transfer to a lightly oiled bowl and set aside for 2 hours or until doubled in size.

Preheat oven to 180°C (350°F). Grease 12 x ¾-cup-capacity (180ml) metal dariole moulds and line the bases with non-stick baking paper. Divide the dough into 12 pieces and roll into balls. Place the balls inside the moulds and place on a large oven tray. Cover with plastic wrap and set aside for 30 minutes or until risen. Remove the plastic wrap and bake for 20 minutes or until golden and cooked through. While still warm, carefully remove the panettones from the moulds and place on a wire rack to cool, before serving. **MAKES 12**
+ *Packets of whole mixed dried fruit are available from the supermarket. You can use your favourite combination.*

butterscotch, peach and ginger individual panettones

hazelnut and brandy forest cake
with cream cheese icing

hazelnut and brandy forest cake with cream cheese icing

225g unsalted butter, chopped and softened
1½ cups (260g) light brown sugar
2 teaspoons vanilla extract
6 eggs
2¼ cups (335g) self-raising (self-rising) flour, sifted
2¼ cups (225g) hazelnut meal (ground hazelnuts)
1 teaspoon ground cinnamon
½ cup (125ml) milk
¼ cup (60ml) brandy, plus 2 tablespoons extra for brushing
gingerbread reindeer, for decorating (see *recipe*, page 224)
1 cup (160g) icing (confectioner's) sugar, sifted, plus extra
    for dusting
2–2½ teaspoons boiling water
3 thick sprigs rosemary
cream cheese icing
500g cream cheese, chopped and softened
100g unsalted butter, chopped and softened
2 cups (320g) icing (confectioner's) sugar, sifted
2 teaspoons vanilla extract

Preheat oven to 160°C (325°F). Line 2 x 18cm round cake tins with non-stick baking paper. Place the butter, sugar and vanilla in the bowl of an electric mixer and beat for 5–6 minutes or until pale and creamy. Add the eggs, 1 at a time, beating well after each addition. Add the flour, hazelnut meal, cinnamon, milk and brandy and beat on low speed until just combined. Divide the mixture evenly between the tins. Bake for 55 minutes – 1 hour or until cooked when tested with a skewer. Allow to cool in the tins for 10 minutes, before turning out onto a wire rack to cool completely.

While the cake is cooling, make the cream cheese icing. Place the cream cheese, butter, sugar and vanilla in a clean bowl of the electric mixer. Beat for 8 minutes or until pale and fluffy[+].

To assemble the cake, trim the tops and slice each cake in half horizontally, using a large serrated knife. Brush each layer of cake with the extra brandy. Place the base of 1 of the cakes on a cake stand or plate and spread with ⅔ cup (160ml) of the icing. Repeat the process 3 more times, finishing with the remaining icing.

To decorate the reindeer, place the icing sugar and boiling water in a small bowl and mix to combine. Spoon into a piping bag fitted with a small round nozzle and pipe spots onto each deer. Top the cake with the rosemary and the reindeer and dust with icing sugar to serve. **SERVES 10–12**
+ *Set the cream cheese icing aside in the refrigerator for 15 minutes if it needs to firm slightly.*

soak the fruit

add the butter mixture

flour the cloth

shape the mixture

tie with kitchen string

lower into the water

christmas pudding

¼ cup (40g) sultanas
½ cup (80g) dried currants
¾ cup (100g) raisins
8 soft fresh dates (160g), pitted and chopped
½ cup (70g) slivered almonds
½ teaspoon mixed spice
⅓ cup (80ml) sweet sherry
⅔ cup (160ml) brandy
125g unsalted butter, softened
¼ cup (45g) light brown sugar
¼ cup (55g) caster (superfine) sugar
2 eggs
⅔ cup (100g) plain (all-purpose) flour, sifted
1½ cups (100g) fresh white breadcrumbs
brandy custard (see *recipe*, page 131), to serve

Place the sultanas, currants, raisins, dates, almonds, mixed spice, sherry and half the brandy in a large bowl and mix to combine. Cover with plastic wrap and allow to soak in a cool, dark place for 24 hours, mixing occasionally.

Place the butter and both the sugars in the bowl of an electric mixer and beat for 8–10 minutes or until pale and creamy. Add the eggs, 1 at a time, beating well after each addition. Add the butter mixture, half the flour and the breadcrumbs to the soaked fruit and mix to combine.

Place a large saucepan of water over high heat and bring to the boil. Add a 60cm-square piece of calico cloth and boil for 5 minutes. Using tongs, remove the calico and allow to cool. Squeeze to remove any excess water. Drain, refill the pan with water and bring to the boil. Open the calico out and top with the remaining ⅓ cup (50g) of flour. Rub the flour over the calico to form a large circle. Spoon the pudding mixture into the centre of the calico to form a mound and gather the ends together firmly. Tie the calico as close to the mixture as possible with kitchen string, leaving at least a 15cm length of string at both ends (see *cook's tips*, page 131). Place the pudding in the water, reduce the heat to medium and cover with a tight-fitting lid. Simmer for 4 hours, adding more water if necessary.

Drain and hang the pudding over a bowl for 24–48 hours or until dry. Cut the string and invert the pudding onto a serving plate. Gently remove the cloth, top with the remaining ⅓ cup (80ml) of brandy and serve with brandy custard. SERVES 6–8

christmas pudding

brandy custard

brandy custard

1½ cups (375ml) milk
1 vanilla bean, halved and seeds scraped
10 egg yolks
⅓ cup (50g) plain (all-purpose) flour
1 cup (160g) icing (confectioner's) sugar, sifted
⅔ cup (160ml) single (pouring) cream, whipped
¼ cup (60ml) brandy

Place the milk and vanilla bean and seeds in a medium saucepan over medium heat and bring just to the boil. Place the egg yolks, flour and sugar in the bowl of an electric mixer and whisk on medium speed until combined. With the motor running, gradually add the milk mixture, whisking until smooth.

Return the mixture to the saucepan over low heat and cook, whisking, for 12–15 minutes or until thickened. Strain into a heatproof bowl, cover the surface with plastic wrap (see *cook's tips*, right) and refrigerate until cold.

When ready to serve the custard, add the whipped cream and gently fold to combine. Add the brandy and stir to combine. Pour into a serving jug to serve. **MAKES 3½ CUPS**

cook's tips

⸰ While English tradition would see families make their puddings on the last Sunday of November and hang them in a cool place until Christmas, warm Australian summers say otherwise! If the weather's warm, it's best to make this pudding up to 2 weeks in advance and store it in the refrigerator. You can reheat the pudding by boiling it for 1 hour or simply removing it from the cloth and microwaving it in single serves.

⸰ The extra lengths of string tied to the pudding make lowering and lifting it a little easier. If your saucepan has two handles you could secure the ends of the string to them to stop the pudding from moving around and catching on the pan. Use the string to hang the pudding to dry, too.

⸰ You can make the custard up to 3 days in advance, however add the whipped cream and brandy just before serving. By placing some plastic wrap over the custard while chilling, you'll prevent a 'skin' from forming on the surface.

cinnamon and candied pecan pavlova

cinnamon and candied pecan pavlova

150ml eggwhite (about 4 eggs) (see *cook's tips*, right)
1 cup (220g) caster (superfine) sugar
1 teaspoon white vinegar
1 cup (250ml) single (pouring) cream
1½ cups (360g) crème fraîche
¼ cup (40g) icing (confectioner's) sugar, plus extra for dusting
1 teaspoon ground cinnamon, plus extra for dusting
candied pecans
1 cup (120g) pecans, toasted
2 tablespoons caster (superfine) sugar
2 tablespoons light brown sugar
2 teaspoons vanilla extract
¼ cup (60ml) whiskey

Preheat oven to 150°C (300°F). Place the eggwhite in the bowl of an electric mixer and whisk on high speed until stiff peaks form. Add the caster sugar, 1 tablespoon at a time, whisking for 30 seconds before adding more. Whisk for a further 6 minutes or until stiff and glossy. Scrape down the sides of the bowl, add the vinegar and whisk for 2 minutes or until glossy and combined. Draw a 26cm circle on a sheet of non-stick baking paper (see *cook's tips*, right) and place on a large baking tray. Spoon 1 cup (250ml) of the meringue into the centre of the circle, leaving a 5cm border. Arrange heaped spoonfuls of the remaining meringue in the border to create a ring. Reduce the oven temperature to 120°C (250°F) and bake for 1 hour 30 minutes or until crisp. Turn the oven off and allow the meringue to cool in the oven with the door closed for 1 hour 30 minutes.

To make the candied pecans, line a baking tray with non-stick baking paper. Place a small saucepan over medium heat. Add the pecans, both the sugars, the vanilla and whiskey and cook, stirring occasionally in the last 1 minute, for 6–7 minutes or until golden and caramelised. Working quickly, carefully pour the mixture onto the tray. Spread and allow to cool completely. Roughly chop and set aside.

Place the cream, crème fraîche and the icing sugar in a clean bowl of the electric mixer and whisk until stiff peaks form. Add the cinnamon and fold to combine. Place the pavlova on a cake stand or plate, top the centre with the cream and sprinkle with the pecans. Dust with extra icing sugar and cinnamon to serve. **SERVES 8–10**

cook's tips

○ Making meringue is a science – for success, be sure to measure the eggwhites carefully (as instructed in the recipe), remembering that egg sizes do vary.

○ When separating the eggs, take care to ensure no yolk escapes into the whites. Egg yolks contain fat, which can prevent the whites from whipping well. For this reason, it's also important to use very clean equipment to beat the eggwhites.

○ Be sure to use fresh, room-temperature eggs – this will help the eggwhites to become more voluminous when beaten.

○ When the mixture is 'stiff and glossy', the sugar should be completely dissolved. To test this, simply rub a little of the mixture between your fingertips. If it feels gritty, continue to whisk.

○ To shape meringue into measured rounds for desserts like pavlova and bombe Alaska, draw circles on the non-stick baking paper to guide you. Use a pencil, then place the paper pencil-side down on the tray to ensure no marks transfer to the meringue.

○ To avoid cracking larger meringues and pavlovas as you move them onto cake stands or plates, use the baking paper below to help you and simply trim any visible paper before serving. You could also try baking meringue on an ovenproof serving plate.

raspberry and eggnog bombe alaska

150ml eggwhite (about 4 eggs) (see *cook's tips*, page 133)
1½ cups (240g) icing (confectioner's) sugar, sifted
500ml store-bought raspberry sorbet, softened
1 litre store-bought vanilla ice-cream
½ cup (140g) store-bought thick vanilla custard
¼ teaspoon each grated nutmeg and ground cinnamon
meringue icing
1½ cups (330g) caster (superfine) sugar
¼ teaspoon cream of tartar
½ cup (125ml) water
150ml eggwhite (about 4 eggs) (see *cook's tips*, page 133)

Preheat oven to 120°C (250°F). Draw an 18cm circle on each of 2 sheets of non-stick baking paper (see *cook's tips*, page 133) and place each on a baking tray. Place the eggwhite in the bowl of an electric mixer and whisk on high speed until stiff peaks form. Add the sugar, 1 tablespoon at a time, whisking for 30 seconds before adding more. Scrape down the sides of the bowl and beat for a further 6 minutes or until stiff and glossy. Spoon into a piping bag fitted with a 2cm round nozzle. Pipe the meringue onto the trays in a spiral to fill in the circles, leaving 5mm of room to spread. Bake for 1 hour or until just crisp. Turn the oven off and allow the meringues to cool in the oven with the door closed for 30 minutes.

Line a deep-sided loose-based 20cm round tin with non-stick baking paper. Place 1 meringue round in the base of the tin+. Spoon in the sorbet and spread evenly. Freeze for 30 minutes or until just set. Scoop the ice-cream into a bowl of the electric mixer and beat on low speed for 1 minute or until softened. Add the custard, nutmeg and cinnamon and beat to combine. Spoon into the tin, reserving 1 cup (250ml), and spread evenly. Top with the remaining meringue round and spread with the reserved ice-cream mixture. Freeze for 6 hours or overnight, until frozen.

To make the meringue icing, place 1¼ cups (275g) of the sugar, the cream of tartar and water in a small saucepan over high heat and stir with a metal spoon until just combined. Bring to the boil, reduce the heat to medium and cook for 4 minutes. Place the eggwhite in a clean bowl of the electric mixer and whisk on high speed until soft peaks form. Add the remaining ¼ cup (55g) sugar in 2 batches and whisk until stiff peaks form. With the motor running, add the sugar syrup in a thin, steady stream and whisk for 2–3 minutes or until thick and glossy.

Remove the cake from the tin and place on a cake stand or plate. Spread the icing over the top and sides, using a palette knife to create swirls and peaks. Use a small kitchen blowtorch to brown the icing to serve++. **SERVES 8-10**

+ *If the meringue rounds for the bombe Alaska are too large, trim them with a small sharp knife to fit the tin.*
++ *You can serve the bombe Alaska immediately, or keep it, un-iced, in the freezer for up to 3 days. Make the meringue icing before serving, remove the cake from the tin, then ice and brown the bombe as instructed.*
Tip: A small blowtorch is a handy tool to have in your kitchen, making light work of super impressive desserts. Find them at kitchenware stores and online.

raspberry and eggnog bombe alaska

peach and raspberry meringue tart

peach and raspberry meringue tart

12 sheets frozen filo (phyllo) pastry, thawed
100g unsalted butter, melted
½ cup (110g) caster (superfine) sugar, plus 2 tablespoons extra
¼ cup (90g) honey
1 vanilla bean, split and seeds scraped
800g peaches, halved and cut into 1cm-thick slices
250g raspberries
meringue topping
225ml eggwhite (about 6 eggs) (see *cook's tips*, page 133)
1½ cups (330g) caster (superfine) sugar
1½ teaspoons white vinegar

Preheat oven to 140°C (275°F). Line a 24cm x 36cm Swiss roll tin with non-stick baking paper. Brush 1 sheet of pastry with butter, sprinkle with 2 teaspoons of the sugar and top with another sheet of pastry. Repeat with the remaining butter, sugar and pastry, finishing with a layer of sugar. Place the pastry stack in the tin. Bake for 20–25 minutes or until golden⁺. Set aside.

Place a large non-stick frying pan over high heat. Add the extra sugar, the honey, vanilla seeds and peaches and cook, stirring frequently, for 1–2 minutes or until the peaches are just soft. Add the raspberries, toss to combine and set aside.

To make the meringue topping, place the eggwhite in the bowl of an electric mixer and whisk on high speed until stiff peaks form. Add the sugar, 1 tablespoon at a time, whisking for 30 seconds before adding more. Whisk for a further 6 minutes or until stiff and glossy. Scrape down the sides of the bowl, add the vinegar and whisk for 2 minutes or until glossy.

Preheat oven grill (broiler) to high. Spoon the meringue into a piping bag fitted with a 2cm round nozzle. Spoon the fruit onto the pastry, reserving the juices. Pipe the meringue onto the fruit and place the tart under the grill for 2–3 minutes or until just golden. Carefully remove the tart from the tin. Drizzle with the reserved juices and slice to serve. **SERVES 8–10**

⁺ *The pastry will have puffed up in the oven but will deflate once it begins to cool.*

maple pavlova roll with poached pears and brandy cream

1 cup (250ml) double (thick) cream
1½ tablespoons brandy
2 tablespoons icing (confectioner's) sugar, plus extra for dusting
150ml eggwhite (about 4 eggs) (see *cook's tips*, page 133)
¾ cup (165g) caster (superfine) sugar
1 teaspoon white vinegar
2 tablespoons maple syrup
poached pears
1½ cups (375ml) water
1½ cups (330g) caster (superfine) sugar
½ cup (125ml) maple syrup
8 baby pears, peeled with stems intact

To poach the pears, place the water, sugar and maple syrup in a large saucepan over low heat and cook, stirring, until the sugar is dissolved. Increase the heat to medium, add the pears and simmer for 20 minutes or until cooked through. Remove the pears from the syrup and set aside. Cook the syrup for a further 10 minutes or until reduced by half. Return the pears to the syrup and set aside to cool.

Preheat oven to 160°C (325°F). Line a 24cm x 36cm Swiss roll tin with non-stick baking paper. Place the cream, brandy and icing sugar in the bowl of an electric mixer and whisk until stiff peaks form. Refrigerate until needed.

Place the eggwhite in a clean bowl of the electric mixer and whisk on high speed until stiff peaks form. Add the caster sugar, 1 tablespoon at a time, whisking for 30 seconds before adding more. Scrape down the sides of the bowl. Add the vinegar and maple syrup and whisk for a further 5 minutes or until glossy. Spoon the meringue mixture into the tin and bake for 20 minutes or until crisp to the touch. Allow to cool in the tin for 3–4 minutes. Gently turn the meringue out onto a wire rack lined with non-stick baking paper and allow to cool to room temperature.

Carefully remove the paper from the meringue and spread the brandy cream lengthways down the centre. Fold both sides of the meringue in to enclose. Place on a serving plate and dust with the extra icing sugar. Slice and serve with the pears and syrup. **SERVES 6–8**

maple pavlova roll with poached pears and brandy cream

chocolate-hazelnut pavlova with marinated raspberries

chocolate-hazelnut pavlova with marinated raspberries

150ml eggwhite (about 4 eggs) (see *cook's tips*, page 133)
1¾ cups (280g) icing (confectioner's) sugar, sifted,
    plus extra for dusting
1 tablespoon cornflour (cornstarch), sifted
1 cup (100g) hazelnut meal (ground hazelnuts)
2 tablespoons cocoa powder, sifted
3½ cups (875ml) single (pouring) cream
200g dark chocolate, chopped
2 cups (500g) mascarpone
marinated raspberries
250g raspberries
1 tablespoon icing (confectioner's) sugar
2 tablespoons white rum

To marinate the raspberries, place the raspberries, sugar and
rum in a small bowl. Mix gently to combine and set aside.

Preheat oven to 120°C (250°F). Draw 2 x 18cm circles on each
of 2 sheets of non-stick baking paper (see *cook's tips*, page 133)
and place each sheet on a baking tray. Place the eggwhite in
the bowl of an electric mixer and whisk on high speed until stiff
peaks form. Add 1½ cups (240g) of the sugar, 1 tablespoon at
a time, whisking for 30 seconds before adding more. Scrape
down the sides of the bowl and whisk for a further 5–7 minutes
or until the mixture is thick and glossy. Add the cornflour,
hazelnut meal and cocoa and whisk until well combined.
Divide the mixture between the circles on the trays and use
a palette knife to spread evenly. Bake for 30 minutes or until
just crisp to the touch. Turn the oven off. Allow the meringues
to cool in the oven with the door closed for 30 minutes. Set
aside to cool completely at room temperature.

Place 1½ cups (375ml) of the cream in a small saucepan
over high heat and bring to the boil. Remove from the heat,
add the chocolate and stir until smooth. Allow to cool completely.

Place the chocolate mixture and mascarpone in a clean
bowl of the electric mixer and whisk until stiff peaks form.
Place the remaining 2 cups (500ml) of cream and ¼ cup (40g)
of sugar in a separate bowl and whisk until soft peaks form.

Place 1 meringue round on a cake stand or plate. Top with
one-third of the chocolate mixture and one-third of the cream
mixture. Repeat twice more. Top with the final meringue round
and the raspberries. Dust with extra sugar to serve. SERVES 8

pandoro and vanilla bombe alaska

1 x 1kg store-bought pandoro[+]
¼ cup (60ml) sloe gin[++]
3 litres store-bought vanilla ice-cream, softened
2 cups (260g) frozen raspberries
italian meringue
⅓ cup (80ml) water
½ teaspoon cream of tartar
2 cups (440g) caster (superfine) sugar
150ml eggwhite (about 4 eggs) (see *cook's tips*, page 133)

Using a large serrated knife, slice about 2cm from the base
of the pandoro. Using a 13cm round plate as a guide, trim and
reserve the base. Using the same plate as a guide and leaving
a 2cm-thick edge, cut into the underside of the cake and
remove the centre to make a hollow. Brush the inside of the
pandoro with the gin.

Line a tray with non-stick baking paper. Place the ice-cream
and raspberries in a large bowl and mix to combine. Working
quickly, spoon the ice-cream mixture into the hollow, top with
the reserved base and press to secure. Place the pandoro,
base-down, on the tray and freeze for 3–4 hours or until solid.

To make the Italian meringue, place the water, cream of
tartar and half the sugar in a small saucepan over high heat.
Cook, stirring, until the sugar has dissolved. Bring to the boil,
reduce the heat to medium and cook for 4 minutes. Place the
eggwhite in the bowl of an electric mixer and whisk on high
speed until stiff peaks form. With the motor running, add
the remaining 1 cup (220g) of sugar, 1 tablespoon at a time,
whisking for 30 seconds before adding more. Gradually
add the hot sugar syrup in a thin steady stream and whisk
for a further 4 minutes or until thick, glossy and cooled.

Place the pandoro on a cake stand or plate. Using a palette
knife, spread the meringue over the pandoro. Using a small
kitchen blowtorch, toast the meringue until golden brown.
Serve immediately. SERVES 8

*+ Pandoro, meaning 'golden bread', is an Italian star-shaped
sweet bread, available from delicatessens and Italian grocers.
If you can't find pandoro, you can use plain or fruit panettone.
++ Sloe gin has a fruity flavour which complements this dessert
well. If unavailable, simply omit it from the recipe.*

pandoro and vanilla bombe alaska

raspberry swirl pavlova wreath

raspberry swirl pavlova wreath

225ml eggwhite (about 6 eggs) (see *cook's tips*, page 133)
1½ cups (330g) caster (superfine) sugar
1½ teaspoons white vinegar
2 teaspoons cornflour (cornstarch)
1½ cups (375ml) single (pouring) cream
250g raspberries
2 tablespoons shelled pistachios, finely chopped
1 tablespoon freeze-dried raspberries, finely crushed (optional)+
raspberry swirl
½ cup (65g) frozen raspberries
2 tablespoons caster (superfine) sugar
1 teaspoon vanilla extract

To make the raspberry swirl, place the raspberries, sugar and vanilla in a small saucepan over medium heat and cook, stirring occasionally, for 3–4 minutes or until slightly reduced. Strain into a heatproof bowl, discarding the seeds, and refrigerate until cool.

Preheat oven to 150°C (300°F). Draw a 22cm circle on a sheet of non-stick baking paper (see *cook's tips*, page 133) and place it on a baking tray. Place the eggwhite in the bowl of an electric mixer and whisk on high speed until stiff peaks form. Gradually add the sugar, 1 tablespoon at a time, whisking for 30 seconds before adding more. Scrape down the sides of the bowl and whisk for a further 6 minutes or until stiff and glossy. Place the vinegar and cornflour in a small bowl and mix to combine. Add to the meringue and whisk for 2 minutes or until glossy and combined.

Place 12 heaped spoonfuls of the meringue mixture on the tray around the inside of the circle to create a ring. Drizzle the raspberry mixture over the meringue and use a teaspoon to create a swirled effect. Reduce the oven temperature to 120°C (250°F) and bake for 1 hour or until crisp to the touch. Turn the oven off and allow the pavlova to cool completely in the oven with the door closed.

Place the cream in a clean bowl of the electric mixer and whisk until soft peaks form.

Place the pavlova wreath on a cake stand or plate. Top with the cream and sprinkle with the raspberries, chopped pistachios and freeze-dried raspberries to serve. SERVES 6-8
+ *Freeze-dried raspberries are available from select delicatessens and specialty grocers.*

raspberry sweet bread wreath

1 teaspoon dry yeast
2 tablespoons caster (superfine) sugar
½ cup (125ml) lukewarm water
1½ tablespoons warm milk
1½ cups 00 (superfine) flour, plus extra for dusting
1½ tablespoons vegetable oil
¼ cup (40g) dried currants
1 tablespoon finely grated orange rind
1 teaspoon ground cinnamon
milk, for brushing
raw or Demerara sugar, for sprinkling
quick raspberry jam
1½ cups (200g) frozen raspberries
⅔ cup (150) caster (superfine) sugar

Place the yeast, caster sugar, water and milk in a medium bowl and stir to combine. Set aside in a warm place for 5 minutes or until bubbles appear on the surface.

Place the flour, oil, currants, orange rind and cinnamon in a large bowl and make a well in the centre. Add the yeast mixture and mix to form a dough. Turn the dough out onto a lightly floured surface and knead for 5–6 minutes or until smooth and elastic. Place in a lightly oiled bowl, cover with a clean, damp tea towel and allow to stand in a warm place for 1 hour or until doubled in size.

While the dough is proving, make the quick raspberry jam+. Place the raspberries and sugar in a medium non-stick frying pan over high heat and stir until the sugar is dissolved. Bring to the boil and cook, stirring, for 5–6 minutes or until reduced and thickened slightly. Set aside to cool completely.

Preheat oven to 200°C (400°F). Roll the dough out on a lightly floured surface to make a rough 25cm x 55cm rectangle. Spread the dough with the jam and roll up, starting from the long edge, to enclose. Using a sharp knife, cut the rolled dough in half lengthways. Join the top of the 2 pieces together and carefully slide onto a sheet of non-stick baking paper. Twist the 2 lengths together, form a wreath shape and join the ends. Gently transfer the paper to a baking tray. Brush the wreath with milk, sprinkle with raw sugar and bake for 15–20 minutes or until golden and cooked through. Tie with a ribbon and place in the centre of the table to serve. SERVES 10-12
+ *You could also use ½ cup (160g) store-bought raspberry jam.*

raspberry sweet bread wreath

smoked almond and cherry panforte

smoked almond and cherry panforte

1 sheet confectionery rice paper[+], for lining
2½ cups (375g) dried cherries[++]
⅓ cup (80ml) bourbon
¾ cup (110g) plain (all-purpose) flour, sifted
⅓ cup (35g) cocoa powder, sifted
2 teaspoons mixed spice
1½ cups (240g) smoked almonds, roughly chopped
120g dark chocolate, melted
¾ cup (270g) honey
1 cup (220g) white (granulated) sugar
1 vanilla bean, split and seeds scraped

Preheat oven to 160°C (325°F). Line a 20cm round springform tin with non-stick baking paper. Trim the rice paper into a round to fit the base of the tin and place it on top of the baking paper.

Place the cherries and bourbon in a medium saucepan over high heat and cook, stirring frequently, for 4–5 minutes or until the fruit is plump. Set aside to cool slightly.

Place the flour, cocoa, mixed spice, almonds, chocolate and the cherry mixture in a large bowl and mix until just combined.

Place the honey, sugar and vanilla seeds in a small saucepan over medium heat and stir until combined. Bring to the boil and cook for 2 minutes or until the temperature reaches 118°C (244°F) on a sugar (candy) thermometer. Add the honey mixture to the chocolate mixture and stir to combine.

Spoon the mixture into the tin, pressing to even the top. Bake for 40–45 minutes or until the panforte is set on the sides and slightly soft in the centre. Allow to cool in the tin for 5 hours or overnight.

Run a small knife around the edge before removing the panforte from the tin. Slice into wedges to serve. SERVES 12
+ You can find confectionery rice paper in the Asian or baking sections of the supermarket or at Asian grocers.
++ You can use sweetened dried cranberries in place of cherries if you prefer.
Tip: Keep the panforte wrapped in plastic wrap in a cool, dark place for up to 2 weeks or refrigerated for up to 1 month. Bring to room temperature before serving.

chocolate christmas cake with quince glaze

1½ cups (260g) pitted prunes
1½ teaspoons bicarbonate of (baking) soda
1 cup (250ml) boiling water
1½ cups (240g) dried currants
¾ cup (180ml) rum
85g unsalted butter, softened
1 teaspoon vanilla extract
1½ cups (260g) light brown sugar
1½ tablespoons finely grated orange rind
6 eggs
1½ cups (225g) self-raising (self-rising) flour, sifted
⅓ cup (35g) cocoa powder, sifted
1½ teaspoons ground cinnamon
½ teaspoon ground allspice
150g dark chocolate, melted
chocolate quince glaze
300g store-bought quince jelly
50g dark chocolate, finely chopped

Preheat oven to 160°C (325°F). Grease a 2.75-litre-capacity bundt tin. Place the prunes, bicarbonate of soda and water in a medium bowl, mix to combine and allow to stand for 10–15 minutes. Using a hand-held stick blender, blend the mixture into a puree and set aside.

Place the currants and rum in a small saucepan over high heat. Cook, stirring, for 5–6 minutes or until plump. Set aside.

Place the butter, vanilla, sugar and orange rind in the bowl of an electric mixer and beat for 10–12 minutes or until combined. Scrape down the sides of the bowl. Add the eggs, 1 at a time, beating well after each addition. Add the flour, cocoa, cinnamon, allspice, chocolate and the fruit mixtures. Beat to combine.

Pour the mixture into the tin and bake for 1 hour or until cooked when tested with a skewer. Invert the cake onto a wire rack and allow to cool in the tin for 10–15 minutes. Remove the tin and allow to cool completely.

To make the chocolate quince glaze, place the quince jelly in a small saucepan over medium heat and whisk until melting. Add the chocolate and whisk to combine. Bring to the boil and cook, whisking, for 2–3 minutes or until thickened. Allow to cool at room temperature.

Place the cake on a cake stand or plate and pour the glaze over just before serving. SERVES 12-14

chocolate christmas cake with quince glaze

spiced chocolate fudge

spiced chocolate fudge

1 cup (250ml) double (thick) cream
¾ cup (180ml) sweetened condensed milk
1 cup (250ml) light corn syrup[+]
1 cup (220g) caster (superfine) sugar
¼ cup (60ml) water
60g unsalted butter, chopped
2 teaspoons ground star-anise[++]
200g dark chocolate, finely chopped

Line a 20cm square cake tin with non-stick baking paper.
Place the cream and condensed milk in a small saucepan over
low heat and stir until just warm. Set aside and keep warm.
   Place the light corn syrup, sugar and water in a medium
saucepan over high heat and stir until the sugar is dissolved.
Bring to the boil and cook, without stirring, until the
temperature reaches 120°C (248°F) on a sugar (candy)
thermometer. Reduce the heat to medium, add the butter,
star-anise and the cream mixture and cook, stirring constantly,
until the temperature reaches 118°C (244°F). Immediately
remove the mixture from the heat, add the chocolate and
stir to combine. Carefully pour into the tin, tapping it
gently to even the surface. Allow the fudge to cool at room
temperature for 2–3 hours or until set.
   Remove the fudge from the tin and slice into pieces to
serve. MAKES 32
+ *Find light corn syrup in specialty food stores and delicatessens.*
++ *Buy ground star-anise in Asian grocers, spice shops and online.*
*Tip: This fudge does not need to be refrigerated. Store it in an
airtight container in a cool, dry place for up to 1–2 weeks.*

spiced chocolate ice-cream slice

¾ cup (180ml) water
100g unsalted butter, chopped
¼ cup (25g) cocoa powder, sifted
1½ cups (225g) plain (all-purpose) flour, sifted
¾ teaspoon bicarbonate of (baking) soda, sifted
½ teaspoon finely grated nutmeg
½ teaspoon ground cinnamon
1½ cups (330g) caster (superfine) sugar
2 eggs
⅓ cup (80ml) buttermilk
1 teaspoon vanilla extract
1½ tablespoons whiskey
1 litre store-bought chocolate ice-cream

Preheat oven to 160°C (325°F). Line a 22cm square cake
tin with non-stick baking paper. Place the water, butter and
cocoa in a medium saucepan over medium heat and stir until
the butter is melted. Transfer to a large bowl and add the flour,
bicarbonate of soda, nutmeg, cinnamon and sugar and mix to
combine. Add the eggs, buttermilk, vanilla and whiskey and
whisk until well combined. Pour into the tin and bake for
45–50 minutes or until cooked when tested with a skewer.
Allow to cool in the tin for 10 minutes before turning out
onto a wire rack to cool completely.
   Using a large serrated knife, trim to even the top of the cake
and halve it horizontally. Re-line the cleaned tin with non-stick
baking paper and add 1 half of the cake. Freeze until ready to
use. Scoop the ice-cream into the bowl of an electric mixer
and beat on low speed for 1–2 minutes or until softened. Spoon
the ice-cream into the tin and spread evenly. Top with the
remaining cake and freeze for 6 hours or overnight, until firm.
Remove the slice from the tin, allow to stand for 1–2 minutes
and trim the edges. Cut into squares to serve. MAKES 16

spiced chocolate ice-cream slice

cinnamon and chocolate caramel apples

cinnamon and chocolate caramel apples

10 wooden sticks
10 small red apples, washed and dried
1 cup (120g) chopped pecans, roasted
1½ cups (375ml) light corn syrup+
300g unsalted butter, chopped
2 cups (220g) caster (superfine) sugar
2 teaspoons ground cinnamon
200g dark chocolate, chopped

Line a baking tray with non-stick baking paper. Push a stick into the centre of each apple and set aside. Place the pecans in a shallow bowl and set aside.

Place 1 cup (250ml) of the light corn syrup, the butter, sugar and cinnamon in a medium saucepan over medium heat and stir until combined. Bring to the boil and cook, without stirring, for 8–10 minutes or until the temperature reaches 140°C (284°F) on a sugar (candy) thermometer. Remove from the heat, add the chocolate and the remaining ½ cup (125ml) of light corn syrup and stir until smooth.

Working quickly, dip the apples into the caramel to coat and press the bases into the pecans. Place on the tray and allow to stand for 30 minutes or until set, before serving. **MAKES 10**
+ *Find light corn syrup in specialty food stores and delicatessens.*

gingerbread men ice-cream sandwiches

4 litres store-bought vanilla ice-cream
125g unsalted butter, chopped and softened
½ cup (90g) light brown sugar
⅔ cup (230g) golden syrup
2½ cups (375g) plain (all-purpose) flour, sifted
2 teaspoons ground ginger
1 teaspoon bicarbonate of (baking) soda

Scoop the ice-cream into the bowl of an electric mixer and beat on low speed until softened. Spoon into a 25cm x 35cm baking dish and smooth the top. Cover with non-stick baking paper and freeze for 3–4 hours or until set.

Place the butter and sugar in a clean bowl of the electric mixer and beat for 8–10 minutes or until pale and creamy. Add the golden syrup, flour, ginger and bicarbonate of soda and beat until the mixture just comes together to form a smooth dough. Roll the dough out between 2 sheets of non-stick baking paper to 4mm thick and refrigerate for 30 minutes.

Preheat oven to 190°C (375°F). Line 2 baking trays with non-stick baking paper. Using a 12cm gingerbread-man-shaped cutter, cut 16 shapes from the dough. Place on the trays and bake for 8–10 minutes or until golden. Allow to cool on the trays.

Lightly grease the cutter and cut 8 men from the ice-cream. Working quickly, sandwich the ice-cream between the cooled cookies and freeze until ready to serve. **MAKES 8**
Tip: You will have gingerbread cookie dough left over. Either wrap it in plastic wrap and freeze for up to 2 months for later use, or roll it out and cut into shapes to bake with the gingerbread men.

gingerbread men ice-cream sandwiches

brandy and maple ice-cream pandoro

brandy and maple ice-cream pandoro

½ cup (125ml) maple syrup
2 tablespoons brandy
1 litre store-bought vanilla ice-cream
1 x 1kg store-bought pandoro or panettone+
icing (confectioner's) sugar, for dusting

Place the maple syrup in a small saucepan over high heat and bring to the boil. Cook for 3–5 minutes or until thickened slightly. Remove from the heat, carefully add the brandy and stir to combine. Set aside to cool.

Scoop the ice-cream into the bowl of an electric mixer and beat on low speed until softened. Add the maple mixture and beat to combine.

Line a tray with non-stick baking paper. Using a large serrated knife, slice about 2cm from the base of the pandoro. Using a 13cm round plate as a guide, trim and reserve the base. Using the same plate as a guide and leaving a 2cm-thick edge, cut into the underside of the cake and remove the centre to make a hollow. Working quickly, spoon the ice-cream mixture into the hollow, top with the reserved base and press to secure. Place the pandoro, base-down, on the tray and freeze for 3–4 hours or until solid.

Place the pandoro on a cake stand or plate and dust with icing sugar to serve. **SERVES 6–8**
+ *Pandoro and panettone are Italian-style, bread-like cakes traditionally served at Christmas. The pandoro is typically star-shaped while the panettone can be more rounded or even mushroom-shaped. Both are found in Italian and specialty grocery stores.*

sour cherry, ginger and pistachio ice-cream tart

500g store-bought ginger nut biscuits+
180g unsalted butter, melted
¼ cup (35g) dried sour cherries
¼ cup (40g) dried currants
½ cup (65g) sweetened dried cranberries
¼ cup (55g) glacé ginger, chopped
¼ cup (35g) slivered pistachios
1½ tablespoons warm brandy
500ml store-bought vanilla ice-cream

Lightly grease an 11cm x 34cm loose-based fluted tart tin. Place the biscuits in a food processor and process until the mixture resembles coarse breadcrumbs. Add the butter and process until well combined. Reserve and set aside 1½ cups of the crumb mixture. Use the back of a spoon to press the remaining crumbs into the base and sides of the tin. Refrigerate for 1 hour or until set.

Place the cherries, currants, cranberries, ginger, pistachios and brandy in a large bowl. Mix to combine and set aside for 20 minutes.

Scoop the ice-cream into the bowl of an electric mixer and beat on low speed until softened. Add the fruit mixture to the ice-cream and fold to combine. Spoon into the tart shell, smooth the top and freeze for 3–4 hours or until set.

Remove the tart from the tin. Sprinkle with the reserved crumb mixture and slice to serve. **SERVES 8**
+ *Ginger nut, or ginger snap, biscuits can vary in texture – you need the super crunchy hard (not chewy) ones for this recipe, to achieve a lovely crisp tart shell.*

sour cherry, ginger and pistachio ice-cream tart

honeycomb and caramel ice-cream trifle

honeycomb and caramel ice-cream trifle

120g store-bought sponge cake, crumbled
2 tablespoons sweet sherry
1 litre store-bought vanilla ice-cream
160g store-bought plain chocolate biscuits (about 16 biscuits)
½ cup (150g) store-bought thick caramel or dulce de leche
100g honeycomb pieces[+]

Line a 2-litre-capacity rectangular tin with non-stick baking paper. Place the cake and sherry in a medium bowl, mix to combine and set aside until the sherry is absorbed.

Scoop one-third of the ice-cream into the bowl of an electric mixer and beat on low speed until softened. Add the soaked cake and gently fold to combine. Spoon into the tin, smooth the top and layer with half the biscuits, overlapping them slightly. Freeze for 1 hour or until just set.

Scoop half the remaining ice-cream into the bowl of the electric mixer. Add the caramel and beat on low speed until softened and combined. Spoon into the tin and smooth to cover the biscuits. Layer with the remaining biscuits and freeze for a further 1–2 hours or until just set.

Place the honeycomb in a small food processor and process until very fine. Scoop the remaining ice-cream into the bowl of the electric mixer and add the honeycomb. Beat on low speed until softened and combined. Spoon into the tin, smooth the top and freeze for a further 3–4 hours or until completely set.

Remove the trifle from the tin and slice to serve. SERVES 6–8
+ Find honeycomb at confectionery stores and specialty grocers, or make your own using the recipe on page 169.

fig and date ice-cream cake with brandy syrup

3 soft fresh dates (60g), pitted and roughly chopped
¼ cup (50g) dried figs, roughly chopped
½ teaspoon bicarbonate of (baking) soda
⅓ cup (80ml) boiling water
60g unsalted butter, softened
½ teaspoon vanilla extract
½ cup (90g) light brown sugar
2 eggs
⅔ cup (100g) self-raising (self-rising) flour, sifted
¼ cup (30g) almond meal (ground almonds)
1½ tablespoons golden syrup
¼ cup (35g) slivered pistachios
2 litres store-bought vanilla ice-cream
brandy syrup
1 cup (220g) caster (superfine) sugar
1 cup (250ml) brandy
½ cup (125ml) water
1 cup (180g) semi-dried baby figs

To make the brandy syrup, place the sugar, brandy and water in a medium saucepan over low heat and cook, stirring, until the sugar is dissolved. Increase the heat to high, bring to the boil and cook for 8–10 minutes or until syrupy. Add the baby figs and set aside to cool completely.

Place the dates, dried figs, bicarbonate of soda and water in a small bowl. Allow to soak for 15 minutes. Place in a food processor and process until smooth.

Preheat oven to 160°C (325°F). Line a deep 20cm round springform tin with non-stick baking paper. Place the butter, vanilla and sugar in the bowl of an electric mixer and beat for 2–3 minutes or until pale and creamy. Add the eggs, 1 at a time, beating well after each addition. Add the flour, date mixture, almond meal, golden syrup and pistachios and beat to combine. Spoon into the tin and bake for 40–45 minutes or until cooked when tested with a skewer. Allow the cake to cool in the tin for 10 minutes. Turn out onto a wire rack to cool completely.

Re-line the cleaned tin. Scoop the ice-cream into the bowl of an electric mixer and beat on low speed until softened. Spoon the ice-cream into the tin and smooth the top. Freeze for 3–4 hours or until set. Remove the ice-cream from the tin. Place on a cake stand or plate and top with the cooled cake. Spoon the brandy syrup over and slice to serve. SERVES 8

fig and date ice-cream cake with brandy syrup

raspberry and white chocolate trifle

raspberry and white chocolate trifle

½ cup (125ml) orange liqueur

20 small store-bought sponge finger biscuits
  (see *cook's tips*, page 162)

250g raspberries, to serve

raspberry jelly

1.5 litres cranberry juice

2 tablespoons gelatine powder

1 cup (220g) caster (superfine) sugar

3¾ cups (500g) frozen raspberries

white chocolate ganache

180g white chocolate, finely chopped

1 cup (250ml) single (pouring) cream

mascarpone cream

½ cup (125g) mascarpone

½ cup (80g) icing (confectioner's) sugar, sifted

1 teaspoon vanilla bean paste or vanilla extract

1½ cups (375ml) single (pouring) cream

To make the raspberry jelly, place 1 cup (250ml) of the cranberry juice in a small bowl. Slowly sprinkle with the gelatine and set aside for 5 minutes or until the gelatine is absorbed. Place the remaining juice and the sugar in a large saucepan over medium heat and stir until the sugar is dissolved. Bring to the boil and cook for 1 minute. Remove from the heat, add the gelatine mixture and whisk to combine. Allow to stand for 20 minutes or until cool. Pour into a 4-litre-capacity glass dish and top with the frozen raspberries. Refrigerate for 4–5 hours or overnight until set (see *cook's tips*, page 162).

To make the white chocolate ganache, place the chocolate in a small saucepan over low heat and stir until melted and smooth. Remove from the heat and add ¼ cup (60ml) of the cream in a thin, steady stream, stirring constantly until well combined. Allow to cool slightly and refrigerate until just cold. Place the remaining ¾ cup (180ml) of cream in the bowl of an electric mixer and whisk on high speed until stiff peaks form. Add the cooled chocolate mixture and gently fold to combine.

To make the mascarpone cream, place the mascarpone, sugar, vanilla and cream in the bowl of an electric mixer and whisk until soft peaks form.

To assemble the trifle, spoon the ganache over the jelly and smooth the top, using a palette knife. Place the liqueur in a small shallow bowl. Dip the biscuits in the liqueur and layer them over the ganache. Spoon the mascarpone cream over the biscuits and sprinkle with the fresh raspberries to serve. **SERVES 6–8**

first make the jelly

then whip up the ganache

spoon it onto the set base

spread until smooth

arrange the biscuits

top with cream and berries

cook's tips

○ You can make the raspberry jelly 1–2 days in advance, before proceeding with the ganache, sponge and mascarpone cream layers.

○ Don't hesitate to mix up the flavours in your trifle. Use frozen cherries in the jelly and fresh cherries on top, or try swapping in blueberries or strawberries.

○ Depending on the size of the sponge finger biscuits and your glass trifle bowl, you may need to trim the biscuits to fit.

○ The trick to creating a show-stopping trifle is to keep the layers visible through the glass dish. Try to smooth the ganache as neatly as you can and layer the sponge fingers in a pretty pattern.

○ Using frozen berries
in the jelly layer of
the trifle helps to cool
and set the mixture.

gingerbread, sherry and caramel trifle

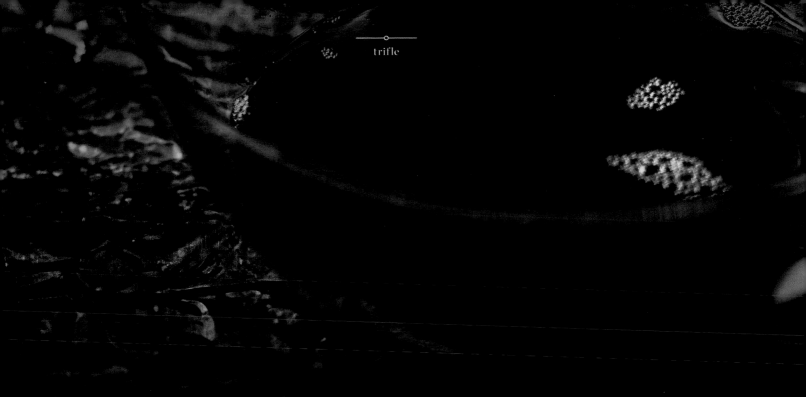

gingerbread, sherry and caramel trifle

3 cups (750ml) single (pouring) cream
3 cups (720g) sour cream
½ cup (150g) store-bought thick caramel or dulce de leche
gingerbread cake
1⅔ cups (250g) plain (all-purpose) flour, sifted
2½ teaspoons baking powder, sifted
2 teaspoons ground ginger
1 teaspoon mixed spice
1 cup (175g) dark brown sugar
125g unsalted butter, chopped
½ cup (175g) golden syrup
½ cup (180g) honey
1 egg, lightly beaten
1¼ cups (310ml) milk
pedro ximénez jelly
3 cups (750ml) water
1½ tablespoons gelatine powder
1 cup (250ml) Pedro Ximénez sherry
1 cup (220g) caster (superfine) sugar

To make the gingerbread cake, preheat oven to 180°C (350°F).
Line a 24cm round tin with non-stick baking paper. Place
the flour, baking powder, ginger, mixed spice and sugar in
a large bowl and mix to combine.

Place the butter, golden syrup and honey in a small saucepan
over low heat and stir until melted and smooth. Add the
butter mixture, the egg and milk to the flour mixture and
whisk until smooth. Pour into the tin and bake for 1 hour or
until cooked when tested with a skewer. Turn out onto a wire
rack and allow to cool completely.

To make the Pedro Ximénez jelly, place ½ cup (125ml) of
the water in a small bowl. Slowly sprinkle with the gelatine and
set aside for 5 minutes or until the gelatine is absorbed. Place
the remaining 2½ cups (625ml) of water, the sherry and sugar
in a medium saucepan over medium heat and stir until the
sugar is dissolved. Bring to the boil and cook for 1 minute.
Remove from the heat, add the gelatine mixture and whisk to
combine. Allow to stand for 15 minutes or until cool. Pour into
a 4-litre-capacity glass dish. Refrigerate for 2 hours or until set.

To assemble the trifle, place the cream and sour cream in
the bowl of an electric mixer and whisk until soft peaks form.
Using a large serrated knife, cut the cooled cake in half
horizontally. Trim the cake layers to fit the glass dish. Place
half the cake on top of the jelly. Spoon one-third of the
cream mixture onto the cake and smooth with a palette knife.
Top with the remaining cake and cream mixture. Spoon the
caramel on top and gently fold into the cream to create a
swirled effect. Refrigerate until ready to serve. SERVES 12-14
Tip: You can make the gingerbread cake 1–2 days ahead. The
trifle can be assembled up to 2–3 hours in advance.

coffee and amaretti trifle

200g store-bought amaretti biscuits, crushed
½ cup (125g) mascarpone
1 cup (250ml) single (pouring) cream
¼ cup (40g) icing (confectioner's) sugar, sifted
coffee jelly
2 cups (500ml) water
1½ tablespoons gelatine powder
3 cups (750ml) coffee liqueur
2 x 30ml shots espresso or strong brewed coffee
chocolate ganache
1½ cups (375ml) single (pouring) cream
300g dark chocolate, finely chopped
coffee cream
1 cup (250g) mascarpone
1¼ cups (310ml) single (pouring) cream
⅓ cup (55g) icing (confectioner's) sugar
1 x 30ml shot espresso or strong brewed coffee, cooled

To make the coffee jelly, place ½ cup (125ml) of the water in a small bowl. Slowly sprinkle with the gelatine and set aside for 5 minutes or until the gelatine is absorbed. Place the remaining 1½ cups (375ml) of water, the liqueur and espresso in a medium saucepan over medium heat and cook, stirring, until the sugar has dissolved. Bring to the boil and cook for 1 minute. Remove from the heat, add the gelatine mixture and whisk to combine. Allow to stand for 15 minutes or until cool. Pour into a 5-litre-capacity glass dish. Refrigerate for 2 hours or until set.

To make the chocolate ganache, place the cream in a small saucepan over medium heat and bring to the boil. Remove from the heat, add the chocolate and allow to stand for 5 minutes or until melted. Stir until smooth and set aside to cool.

To make the coffee cream, place the mascarpone, cream, sugar and coffee in the bowl of an electric mixer and whisk until stiff peaks form. Set aside in the refrigerator.

To assemble the trifle, sprinkle the amaretti, reserving ½ cup, over the jelly and top with the coffee cream. Spoon over the ganache and smooth with a palette knife. Refrigerate for 10 minutes or until set. Place the mascarpone, cream and sugar in the bowl of an electric mixer and whisk until soft peaks form. Spoon the cream mixture onto the trifle and sprinkle with the reserved amaretti to serve. **SERVES 10–12**
Tip: This trifle can be assembled up to 2–3 hours ahead. Refrigerate until ready to serve.

coffee and amaretti trifle

brandy eggnog panettone trifle

brandy eggnog panettone trifle

800g store-bought panettone, cut into squares
3 cups (750g) mascarpone
2 cups (500ml) single (pouring) cream
1 tablespoon brandy
½ cup (80g) icing (confectioner's) sugar, sifted,
    plus extra to serve
¼ cup (20g) flaked almonds, toasted
brandy jelly
2½ cups (625ml) water
1 tablespoon gelatine powder
1½ cups (375ml) brandy
1 teaspoon vanilla extract
1¼ cups (275g) caster (superfine) sugar

To make the brandy jelly mixture, place ½ cup (125ml) of the water in a small bowl. Sprinkle with the gelatine and set aside for 5 minutes or until the gelatine is absorbed. Place the remaining 2 cups (500ml) of water, the brandy, vanilla and sugar in a medium saucepan over medium heat and stir until the sugar is dissolved. Bring to the boil and cook, stirring, for 1 minute. Remove from the heat, add the gelatine mixture and whisk to combine. Set aside to cool for 20 minutes.

Arrange the panettone, overlapping slightly, in the base of a 4-litre-capacity glass dish. Pour the cooled jelly mixture over the panettone and refrigerate for 2 hours or until set.

Place the mascarpone, cream, brandy and sugar in the bowl of an electric mixer and whisk until stiff peaks form.

To assemble the trifle, spoon the mascarpone mixture onto the jelly and sprinkle with the almonds. Dust with extra icing sugar to serve. **SERVES 10-12**
Tip: You can assemble this trifle up to 2–3 hours ahead. Refrigerate until ready to serve. Top with the almonds and dust with sugar just before serving.

honeycomb

2 cups (440g) white (granulated) sugar
⅔ cup (160ml) light corn syrup
⅓ cup (80ml) water
1 tablespoon bicarbonate of (baking) soda, sifted

Line a 6cm-deep 20cm x 30cm roasting pan with non-stick baking paper. Place the sugar, light corn syrup and water in a medium saucepan over medium heat and stir to combine. Bring to the boil and cook for 12–14 minutes or until the temperature reaches 152°C (305°F) on a sugar (candy) thermometer. Remove from the heat and, working quickly, add the bicarbonate of soda, whisking until well combined. Immediately pour the mixture into the tin, tilting to spread evenly. Allow to stand for 30 minutes or until cool and set.

Remove the honeycomb from the tin and break into shards to serve. **SERVES 10-12**
Tip: Honeycomb can be stored in an airtight container for 1–2 weeks.

chocolate caramel brittle

450g unsalted butter, chopped
2 cups (440g) white (granulated) sugar
2 tablespoons glucose syrup
½ cup (125ml) water
300g dark chocolate, finely chopped

Line a 24cm x 34cm baking tray with non-stick baking paper. Place the butter in a medium saucepan over medium heat and stir until melted. Add the sugar, glucose syrup and water and stir with a metal spoon to combine. Place a sugar (candy) thermometer in the saucepan and cook, stirring occasionally when the temperature reads above 140°C (284°F), for 22–25 minutes or until it reaches 152°C (305°F). Working quickly, pour the caramel onto the tray and allow to stand for 5 minutes.

Sprinkle the chocolate over the caramel and allow to melt for 2 minutes. Smooth the chocolate using a palette knife and allow to stand at room temperature for 10 minutes. Refrigerate for 40 minutes or until the chocolate is set.

Break the brittle into shards to serve. **SERVES 10-12**
Tip: Store the brittle in an airtight container for up to 1 week.

honeycomb

chocolate caramel brittle

raspberry and vanilla coconut ice

raspberry and vanilla coconut ice

1.28kg icing (confectioner's) sugar, sifted
6 cups (480g) desiccated coconut
½ teaspoon vanilla extract
1½ cups (375ml) sweetened condensed milk
plain (all-purpose) flour, for dusting
1 cup (130g) frozen raspberries, thawed
1–2 drops red food colouring

Line a 20cm x 30cm slice tin with non-stick baking paper. Place 4 cups (640g) of the sugar, 3 cups (240g) of the coconut and the vanilla in a large bowl. Add 1¼ cups (310ml) of the sweetened condensed milk and mix well to combine. Turn the mixture out onto a lightly floured surface and knead until smooth. Press evenly into the base of the tin and set aside.

Place the remaining 4 cups (640g) of sugar and 3 cups (240g) of coconut in a large bowl. Add the raspberries and food colouring and, using your fingers, rub the mixture until the raspberries are well combined. Add the remaining ¼ cup (65ml) of condensed milk and mix to combine. Turn the mixture out onto a lightly floured surface and knead until smooth. Press the raspberry mixture into the tin over the vanilla layer. Cover with plastic wrap and refrigerate for 3–4 hours or until set.

Slice the coconut ice into pieces to serve. MAKES 50
Tip: Keep coconut ice in an airtight container in the refrigerator for up to 2 weeks. Bring to room temperature before serving.

chocolate pecan pie bars

200g dark chocolate, chopped
80g unsalted butter
1 cup (175g) light brown sugar
1 cup (350g) golden syrup
½ cup (125ml) single (pouring) cream
7 eggs
1 cup (200g) chopped candied clementines
3 cups (360g) pecans, roughly chopped
chocolate pastry
¼ cup (25g) cocoa powder
1½ cups (225g) plain (all-purpose) flour
125g cold unsalted butter, chopped
½ cup (80g) icing (confectioner's) sugar
3 egg yolks
1 tablespoon iced water
1 eggwhite

To make the chocolate pastry, line a 30cm x 40cm Swiss roll tin with non-stick baking paper. Place the cocoa, flour, butter and sugar in a food processor and process until the mixture resembles fine breadcrumbs. With the motor running, add the egg yolks and process to combine. Add the water and process until a dough comes together. Turn the dough out and press it into the base of the tin. Smooth the top with the back of a spoon, brush with the eggwhite and refrigerate for 20 minutes or until firm.

Preheat oven to 160°C (325°F). Place the chocolate and butter in a heatproof bowl over a saucepan of simmering water and stir until melted and smooth. Allow to cool slightly.

Place the sugar, golden syrup, cream and eggs in a large bowl. Add the chocolate mixture and whisk until well combined. Add the clementines and mix to combine. Spoon the mixture over the pastry, spread evenly and decorate with the pecans. Bake for 40–45 minutes or until just set. Allow to cool in the tin for 20 minutes. Refrigerate until cold.

Remove the slice from the tin, trim the edges and cut into bars to serve. MAKES 30
Tip: Keep the bars refrigerated in an airtight container for up to 3–4 days.

chocolate pecan pie bars

rocky road

rocky road

1kg dark chocolate, chopped
2 tablespoons vegetable oil
1 cup (130g) sweetened dried cranberries
200g store-bought marshmallows
250g store-bought Turkish delight pieces
1 cup (50g) coconut flakes
1 cup (140g) shelled unsalted pistachios, chopped

Line a 25cm x 32cm slice tin with non-stick baking paper.
Place the chocolate and oil in a large heatproof bowl over a
saucepan of simmering water and stir until melted and smooth.
Place the cranberries, marshmallows, Turkish delight,
coconut and pistachios in a large bowl and mix to combine.
Reserve and set aside 1 cup (250ml) of the melted chocolate.
Add the remaining chocolate to the rocky road mixture and
stir to combine. Spoon the mixture into the tin, pressing
down gently to spread it to the edges. Pour the reserved
chocolate over the rocky road and spread evenly with a
palette knife. Refrigerate for 30 minutes or until set.
Remove the rocky road from the tin and slice into long
bars to serve. MAKES 6
Tips: Store the rocky road in a cool, dry place for up to 1 week.
Wrap bars in paper and tie with ribbon to make sweet edible gifts.

chewy caramels with salted peanuts

3 cups (420g) salted peanuts
1.1kg white (granulated) sugar
1.125 litres single (pouring) cream
1 cup (350g) golden syrup
100g unsalted butter, chopped

Line a 20cm x 30cm slice tin with non-stick baking paper.
Sprinkle the base with half the peanuts and set aside.
Place the sugar, cream, golden syrup and butter in a large
saucepan over high heat and stir with a metal spoon until the
butter and sugar have melted. Reduce the heat to medium
and cook, stirring, for 20–25 minutes or until the temperature
reaches 122°C (251°F) on a sugar (candy) thermometer.
Working quickly, pour the caramel into the tin and carefully
sprinkle with the remaining 1½ cups (210g) of peanuts. Allow
to cool completely at room temperature for 3–4 hours.
Refrigerate for 25–30 minutes or until firm.
Turn the caramel out onto a board and, using a large sharp
knife, cut into pieces⁺. Wrap each caramel in brown wax paper,
twisting the ends to seal. Keep refrigerated and bring to room
temperature to serve. MAKES 50
+ If the caramel becomes too soft to cut, simply return it to the
refrigerator for 5 minutes.
Tip: Store caramels, wrapped in paper, in the refrigerator for up
to 2 weeks.

chewy caramels with salted peanuts

almond, cranberry and nougat bark

350g dark chocolate, melted
⅓ cup (55g) almonds, toasted and chopped
½ cup (75g) sweetened dried cranberries
150g store-bought almond nougat, chopped
50g dark chocolate, melted, extra

Line a large baking tray with non-stick baking paper. Pour
the chocolate onto the tray and, using a palette knife, spread
into a thin layer. Sprinkle with the chopped almonds, the
cranberries and nougat. Refrigerate for 1 hour or until set.

  Using a teaspoon, drizzle with the extra chocolate and
refrigerate for 10 minutes or until set.

  Break the bark into pieces to serve. **SERVES 8**

*Tip: Store the bark in an airtight container in the refrigerator
for up to 3 days.*

frozen coconut and nougat slice

2 litres store-bought vanilla ice-cream, softened
1½ cups (50g) puffed brown rice
1½ cups (110g) shredded coconut, plus extra to serve
200g store-bought almond nougat, finely chopped

Line a 20cm x 30cm slice tin with non-stick baking paper.
Place the ice-cream, puffed rice, coconut and nougat in a
large bowl and, working quickly, mix to combine. Spoon into
the tin and smooth the top with a palette knife. Freeze for
3–4 hours or until firm.

  Remove the slice from the tin and cut into squares.
Sprinkle with extra coconut to serve. **MAKES 20**

nougat, ginger and mascarpone trifles

¾ cup (185g) mascarpone
1¼ cups (310ml) single (pouring) cream
1 teaspoon vanilla extract
200g store-bought almond nougat, thinly sliced
   using a serrated knife
¼ cup (55g) crystallised ginger, finely chopped
store-bought ginger syrup, to serve[+]

Place the mascarpone, cream and vanilla in a medium bowl and whisk until soft peaks form.

Divide the mascarpone mixture, nougat and crystallised ginger between serving glasses to create a layered effect.

Drizzle the trifles with ginger syrup to serve. **MAKES 4**
+ *You can find ginger syrup at specialty grocers or delicatessens. If unavailable, use honey in its place.*

chocolate and raspberry dipped nougat

100g 70% dark chocolate, melted
½ teaspoon vegetable oil
300g store-bought almond nougat, cut into 2cm pieces
1 tablespoon freeze-dried raspberries[+], crushed

Line a small tray with non-stick baking paper. Place the chocolate and oil in a small bowl and mix to combine.

Dip 1 end of each nougat piece into the chocolate mixture, shaking off any excess, and place on the tray. Sprinkle with the crushed raspberries and refrigerate for 15 minutes or until set, before serving. **MAKES 10**
+ *Freeze-dried raspberries are available from selected delicatessens and specialty grocers.*
Tip: Keep the nougat in an airtight container for up to 3 days.

gingerbread and peanut caramel squares

gingerbread and peanut caramel squares

175g unsalted butter, softened
1¼ cups (220g) light brown sugar
½ cup (175g) golden syrup
1 cup (250ml) single (pouring) cream
1½ cups (210g) unsalted peanuts
gingerbread
125g unsalted butter, softened
½ cup (90g) light brown sugar
⅔ cup (230g) golden syrup
2½ cups (375g) plain (all-purpose) flour, sifted
1 teaspoon bicarbonate of (baking) soda, sifted
2 teaspoons ground ginger
2 teaspoons mixed spice

To make the gingerbread, line a 20cm x 30cm slice tin with non-stick baking paper, allowing 3cm of paper to sit above the edges. Place the butter and sugar in the bowl of an electric mixer and beat for 5–6 minutes, scraping down the sides of the bowl, until pale and creamy. Add the golden syrup, flour, bicarbonate of soda, ginger and mixed spice and beat until the mixture just comes together to form a dough. Press the dough into the tin and refrigerate for 30 minutes or until firm.

Preheat oven to 180°C (350°F). Bake the gingerbread for 12–15 minutes or until golden. Set aside to cool in the tin.

Place the butter, sugar and golden syrup in a medium saucepan over medium heat and stir until melted and smooth. Bring to the boil and cook for 8–10 minutes or until the temperature reaches 140°C (284°F) on a sugar (candy) thermometer. Gradually add the cream, stir to combine and cook for 2 minutes. Add the peanuts and stir to combine. Carefully pour the caramel onto the gingerbread base. Place the tin on a large oven tray[+] and bake for 15–18 minutes or until dark golden and slightly set around the edges. Allow to cool in the tin at room temperature for 10 minutes before refrigerating until set.

Use the paper to help you lift the slice from the tin. Using a sharp knife, trim the edges and cut the slice into squares. Keep refrigerated until ready to serve. MAKES 15
+ *It's a good idea to place the tin on a large baking tray in case the caramel bubbles over while cooking.*
Tip: This slice will keep in the refrigerator for up to 2–3 days. Bring it to room temperature to serve.

twisted honey caramels

1 cup (250ml) double (thick) cream
65g unsalted butter, chopped
1⅓ cups (295g) white (granulated) sugar
⅔ cup (240g) honey
sea salt flakes (optional), to serve

Line a 20cm square cake tin with non-stick baking paper[+]. Place the cream and butter in a small saucepan over low heat and stir until the butter is melted. Set aside and keep warm.

Place the sugar and honey in a medium deep-sided saucepan over medium heat and cook, stirring occasionally, until the sugar has dissolved. Bring to the boil and cook, brushing any sugar crystals down the sides of the pan with a wet pastry brush, for 6–7 minutes or until the temperature reaches 154°C (309°F) on a sugar (candy) thermometer. Gradually add the warm cream mixture and mix well to combine[++]. Cook for a further 11–12 minutes or until the temperature reaches 127°C (260°F).

Working quickly, carefully pour the caramel into the tin and allow to stand at room temperature for 4 hours or until firm.

Slice the caramel into 1cm-wide lengths, halve each length and twist the caramels from each end. Wrap in squares of non-stick baking paper and twist the ends to seal. Refrigerate until needed. Sprinkle with sea salt to serve. MAKES 40
+ *It's best to work quickly but carefully when making caramel – line your tin and measure the ingredients before you begin.*
++ *When pouring the cream into the syrup, the hot mixture will boil and bubble – take care and use a deep saucepan.*
Tip: These caramels will keep in the refrigerator for up to 1 week.

twisted honey caramels

black sea salt and chocolate caramel macarons

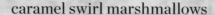
black sea salt and chocolate caramel macarons

1¼ cups (200g) pure icing (confectioner's) sugar
¾ cup (90g) almond meal (ground almonds)
¼ cup (25g) cocoa powder
3 eggwhites, at room temperature
1 tablespoon caster (superfine) sugar
2 teaspoons black sea salt flakes
1 cup (300g) store-bought thick caramel or dulce de leche

Preheat oven to 150°C (300°F). Line 2 large baking trays with non-stick baking paper. Sift the icing sugar, almond meal and cocoa into a large bowl. Mix to combine and set aside.

Place the eggwhites in the bowl of an electric mixer and whisk on high speed for 30 seconds. Add the caster sugar and whisk for 10 minutes or until stiff peaks form and the sugar is dissolved. In 2 batches, add the cocoa mixture and gently fold to combine. Spoon the mixture into a piping bag fitted with a 1.5cm round nozzle and pipe 32 x 4cm rounds onto the trays. Gently tap the trays on a benchtop to remove any air bubbles and allow to stand for 30 minutes or until a skin forms on the surface of the macarons. Sprinkle half the macarons with the salt. Reduce the oven temperature to 130°C (260°F) and bake for 15–18 minutes or until crisp on the outside and chewy in the centre. Allow to cool completely on the trays.

Spoon the caramel onto the underside of the unsalted macarons and sandwich with the remaining macarons to serve. MAKES 16

Tip: These macarons will keep, unfilled, in an airtight container for 1–2 days. Fill them on the day you plan to serve them.

caramel swirl marshmallows

½ cup (125ml) warm water
2 tablespoons gelatine powder
1½ cups (330g) caster (superfine) sugar
⅔ cup (230g) liquid glucose
½ cup (125ml) water, extra
½ cup (150g) store-bought thick caramel or dulce de leche
1 cup (160g) icing (confectioner's) sugar mixture, sifted,
    plus extra for dusting

Line a 20cm x 30cm slice tin with non-stick baking paper, allowing 3cm of paper to sit above the edges. Place the warm water in the bowl of an electric mixer and slowly sprinkle with the gelatine. Set aside for 5 minutes or until the gelatine is absorbed.

Place the caster sugar, glucose and the extra water in a medium saucepan over low heat. Cook, stirring, until the sugar has dissolved. Increase the heat to high and bring to the boil. Cook, without stirring, for 6–7 minutes or until the temperature reaches 115°C (239°F) on a sugar (candy) thermometer.

With the electric mixer on high speed, gradually add the hot syrup to the gelatine mixture in a thin steady stream and whisk for 3 minutes or until thick and glossy. Working quickly, add the caramel and gently fold to combine. Carefully spoon the mixture into the tin. Use a sheet of non-stick baking paper to help you carefully smooth the marshmallow into an even layer. Refrigerate for 1–2 hours or until set.

Use the paper to help you lift the marshmallow from the tin. Dust a large knife with extra icing sugar. Trim the edges and cut the marshmallow into squares. Dust squares with the icing sugar mixture to serve. MAKES 15

Tip: These marshmallows will keep refrigerated in an airtight container for up to 1 week.

caramel swirl marshmallows

fruit mince pies

fruit mince pies

1 Granny Smith (green) apple, peeled and grated
⅔ cup (110g) dried currants
¾ cup (120g) sultanas
½ cup (70g) slivered almonds
⅔ cup (110g) mixed peel
⅓ cup (80ml) maple syrup
½ cup (90g) light brown sugar
60g unsalted butter, chopped
⅓ cup (80ml) butterscotch schnapps or sherry
1 egg, lightly beaten
white (granulated) sugar, for sprinkling
    (see *cook's tips*, page 188)
icing (confectioner's) sugar, for dusting
spiced brown sugar pastry
2⅔ cups (400g) plain (all-purpose) flour,
    plus extra for dusting
300g cold unsalted butter, chopped
½ cup (90g) light brown sugar
½ teaspoon ground ginger
½ teaspoon ground cinnamon
2 eggs
2 teaspoons vanilla extract

To make the spiced brown sugar pastry, place the flour, butter, sugar, ginger and cinnamon in a food processor and process in short bursts until the mixture resembles coarse breadcrumbs. Add the eggs and vanilla and process until the pastry comes together. Turn out onto a generously floured bench and, using your hands, bring the dough together and divide it in half. Generously dust 4 sheets of non-stick baking paper with flour. Roll out each piece of dough between 2 sheets of the paper to 5mm thick. Refrigerate for 30 minutes.

Preheat oven to 160°C (325°F). Place the apple, currants, sultanas, almonds, mixed peel, maple syrup, brown sugar, butter and schnapps in a medium saucepan over medium heat and cook, stirring occasionally, for 15 minutes or until the fruit is softened and the liquid is absorbed. Set aside to cool completely.

Lightly grease 24 x 2-tablespoon-capacity patty tins. Using a 7cm round cookie cutter lightly dusted in flour, cut 24 rounds from the dough (see *cook's tips*, page 188) and use them to line the tins. Re-roll the remaining dough between 2 generously floured sheets of non-stick baking paper to 5mm thick. Refrigerate for a further 15 minutes.

Divide the cooled fruit mixture between the pastry cases and brush the edges of the cases with egg. Using a 7cm fluted cookie cutter lightly dusted in flour, cut 24 rounds from the remaining dough. Using a 1cm round piping nozzle, cut a hole in the centre of each round.

Top the pies with the fluted rounds and press the edges to seal. Brush the tops with egg and sprinkle with the white sugar. Bake for 25–30 minutes or until golden.

Allow the pies to cool in the tins for 5 minutes before turning out onto wire racks to cool completely. Dust with icing sugar to serve. **MAKES 24**

use floured cutters

line and fill the tins

cut pretty fluted tops

press the edges to seal

brush with a little egg

sprinkle with sugar

cook's tips

◦ While you could use a plain sweet shortcrust pastry for this recipe, the brown sugar and spices add a lovely warmth to the overall flavour of the pies.

◦ When making the pastry rounds, be sure to dust the cutters with flour. It makes cutting and lifting a breeze.

◦ If you don't have a fluted cutter, you can use a plain round cutter for the tops. The small hole in the centre is essential though, to let the steam escape while the pies are baking. It prevents the fruit mixture from spilling through the seams.

◦ We use both white, or granulated, sugar and icing, or confectioner's, sugar for dusting – the white sugar before baking adds a lovely crunch and the icing sugar adds extra sweetness.

◦ These fruit pies will keep in an airtight container at room temperature for 2–3 days.

eggnog truffles

eggnog truffles

½ cup (125ml) single (pouring) cream
5 cups (750g) white chocolate melts⁺
¼ cup (60ml) brandy
¼ teaspoon ground cinnamon
¼ teaspoon ground nutmeg
200g store-bought Madeira cake, crumbled
1 tablespoon vegetable oil

Place the cream in a small saucepan over high heat and bring to the boil. Place 1½ cups (225g) of the chocolate melts in a medium heatproof bowl and top with the hot cream. Place the bowl over a saucepan of simmering water and, using a metal spoon, stir until melted and smooth. Remove from the heat, add the brandy and mix to combine.

Place the cinnamon and nutmeg in a small bowl and mix to combine. Place the cake in a food processor. Add the chocolate mixture and half the spice mixture and pulse until smooth and combined. Transfer to a large bowl and refrigerate for 2–3 hours or until firm.

Line a large tray with non-stick baking paper. Roll 1-teaspoon portions of the mixture into balls, place on the tray and freeze for 30 minutes or until firm.

Place the oil and the remaining 3½ cups (525g) of the chocolate melts in a medium heatproof bowl over a saucepan of simmering water. Stir, using a metal spoon, until melted and smooth. Insert a toothpick into each truffle. Dip the truffles in the melted chocolate, allowing any excess to drip off. Stand them in a piece of Styrofoam or thick cardboard. Dust with the remaining spice mixture and refrigerate for 30 minutes or until set.

Remove the toothpicks from the truffles to serve. MAKES 30
⁺ White chocolate melts will set more firmly than regular white chocolate, plus they're easier to melt without the mixture seizing.
Tip: Keep truffles refrigerated until ready to serve.

christmas cake ice-cream truffles

1 cup (250ml) store-bought vanilla ice-cream
200g store-bought Christmas fruit cake, crumbled
400g milk chocolate, finely chopped
1 tablespoon vegetable oil

Line 2 large baking trays with non-stick baking paper and place in the freezer to chill. Scoop the ice-cream into the bowl of an electric mixer and beat on low speed until softened. Add the cake and beat until just combined. Spoon into a loaf tin and freeze for 2 hours or until just set.

Scoop 1-teaspoon portions of the ice-cream mixture into balls, place on the trays and freeze for 1 hour or until firm.

Place the chocolate and oil in a medium heatproof bowl over a saucepan of simmering water and, using a metal spoon, stir until melted and smooth. Allow to stand at room temperature for 10 minutes. Working quickly, insert a toothpick into each truffle. Dip the truffles in the melted chocolate, allowing any excess to drip off and reserving the remaining chocolate. Stand the truffles in a piece of Styrofoam or thick cardboard. Return to the freezer for 10 minutes or until set.

Lightly grease a wire rack and set it over a tray lined with non-stick baking paper. Remove the toothpicks and place the truffles on the rack. Slowly drizzle the remaining chocolate over the truffles, remelting if necessary. Freeze truffles for 10 minutes or until set. Keep frozen until ready to serve. MAKES 25
Tip: These ice-cream truffles will keep, frozen, for up to 2 weeks.

christmas cake ice-cream truffles

coffee amaretti truffles

butterscotch truffles

1 cup (250ml) single (pouring) cream
½ cup (110g) caster (superfine) sugar
¼ cup (60ml) water
50g unsalted butter, chopped
250g dark chocolate, finely chopped
200g 70% dark chocolate, melted⁺
cocoa powder, for dusting (optional)

Place the cream in a small saucepan over medium heat and bring to the boil. Remove from the heat and set aside.

Place the sugar and water in a medium saucepan over low heat and stir until the sugar has dissolved. Increase the heat to medium and bring to the boil. Cook, without stirring, for 6 minutes or until deep golden in colour. Remove from the heat and, working quickly, add the butter and warm cream. Return to the heat and cook, stirring, for 1 minute or until the mixture is smooth and combined. Place the chopped chocolate in a medium heatproof bowl. Top with the caramel mixture and stir until melted and smooth. Allow to stand at room temperature for 10 minutes. Refrigerate for 2–3 hours or until set.

Line a large tray with non-stick baking paper. Roll 1-teaspoon portions of the truffle mixture into balls and place on the tray. Freeze for 1 hour or until firm.

Insert a toothpick into each truffle. Dip into the melted chocolate, allowing any excess to drip off. Stand the truffles in a piece of Styrofoam or thick cardboard. Refrigerate for 1 hour or until set.

Remove the toothpicks from the truffles and dust with cocoa to serve. **MAKES 40**
+ *70% dark chocolate has a lower fat content than regular chocolate, making it the perfect choice for a bittersweet, crispy coating. We've used regular dark chocolate to create the smooth, creamy filling.*
Tip: Keep truffles refrigerated until ready to serve.

coffee amaretti truffles

¾ cup (180ml) single (pouring) cream
¼ cup (10g) good-quality instant coffee granules
600g dark chocolate, finely chopped
¼ cup (60ml) coffee liqueur
4 cups (200g) crushed amaretti biscuits
¼ cup (20g) coffee beans (optional)

Place the cream and instant coffee granules in a small saucepan over high heat and bring to the boil. Place the chocolate in a medium heatproof bowl and top with the hot cream mixture. Place the bowl over a saucepan of simmering water and, using a metal spoon, stir until melted and smooth. Add the liqueur and mix to combine. Allow to cool at room temperature for 10 minutes. Refrigerate for 2–3 hours or until just firm.

Line a large tray with non-stick baking paper. Spread the crushed amaretti on a medium plate. Roll 1-teaspoon portions of the chocolate mixture into balls and roll in the amaretti, pressing to coat. Decorate each truffle with a coffee bean and place on the tray. Refrigerate for 30 minutes or until firm.

Keep truffles refrigerated until ready to serve. **MAKES 45**

butterscotch truffles

candy cane white chocolate bars

500g store-bought plain shortbread biscuits
180g unsalted butter, melted
360g white chocolate, melted
2 teaspoons vegetable oil
6 candy canes, coarsely crushed (see *note*, right)

Line a 20cm x 30cm slice tin with non-stick baking paper.
Place the biscuits in a food processor and process until fine.
Add the butter and process until combined. Transfer to the
tin and, using the back of a spoon, press the mixture evenly
into the base. Refrigerate for 15–20 minutes or until firm.

 Place the chocolate and oil in a small bowl and mix to
combine. Pour the chocolate over the biscuit base. Allow
to stand for 5 minutes or until just starting to set. Sprinkle
with the crushed candy cane and refrigerate for 1–2 hours or
until firm. Allow to stand at room temperature for 5 minutes
before cutting into bars with a hot knife to serve. **SERVES 4–6**

candy cane milkshakes

2 candy canes, finely crushed[+]
180g white chocolate, melted and cooled slightly
1 cup (250ml) cold milk
4 scoops (240ml) store-bought vanilla ice-cream
½ cup (125ml) single (pouring) cream, whipped to stiff peaks

Place the crushed candy canes on a small plate. Dip the rim
of 4 x ¾-cup-capacity (180ml) serving glasses into the
chocolate and press into the crushed candy cane. Place the
glasses upside-down on a tray until the chocolate has set.

 Place the milk, ice-cream and the remaining chocolate in a
blender and blend until smooth. Divide the milkshake between
the prepared glasses and top with the cream to serve. **MAKES 4**
+ *The best way to crush the candy canes is to place them in a
plastic sandwich bag and pound with a meat mallet or rolling pin to
the desired size. Humidity can affect the candy canes, making them
quite sticky once crushed. It helps to crush them just before use.*

candy cane and brownie ice-cream

2 litres store-bought vanilla ice-cream
100g store-bought chocolate brownie (about 1 brownie),
   roughly chopped
8 candy canes, coarsely crushed (see *note*, page 196)

Place a 2-litre-capacity metal container in the freezer until
ready to use.

Scoop the ice-cream into the bowl of an electric mixer
and beat on low speed for 1–2 minutes or until softened.
Add the brownie and three-quarters of the crushed candy
cane and fold to combine. Spoon into the chilled tin.
Sprinkle the ice-cream with the remaining crushed candy
cane and freeze for 3–4 hours or until set. **MAKES 2 LITRES**

cookies and cream candy cane truffles

10 candy canes
300g store-bought cream-filled chocolate biscuits
400g dark chocolate, melted
2 teaspoons vanilla extract
⅓ cup (80ml) single (pouring) cream

Place the candy canes in a food processor and process until
ground. Remove 2 tablespoons of the mixture and set aside.

Add the biscuits to the processor with the remaining candy
cane and process until finely ground. Add half the chocolate
and the vanilla and process until well combined. Add the
cream and process until just combined. Transfer the mixture
to a medium bowl and refrigerate for 15 minutes or until firm.

Line a tray with non-stick baking paper. Roll 1-tablespoon
portions of the mixture into balls and dip into the remaining
chocolate, remelting if necessary. Place the truffles on the
tray and sprinkle with the reserved candy cane. Refrigerate
for 1 hour or until set, before serving. **MAKES 30**

process to make a dough

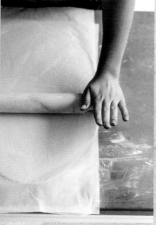
roll out half the dough

use star-shaped cutters

press the remaining dough

spread the base with jam

top with overlapping stars

raspberry and shortbread slice

250g cold unsalted butter, chopped
1 cup (160g) icing (confectioner's) sugar, sifted,
   plus extra for dusting
1½ cups (225g) plain (all-purpose) flour, sifted
½ cup (90g) white rice flour, sifted
   (see *cook's tips*, page 201)
1 teaspoon vanilla extract
1 x quantity cheat's raspberry jam, cooled
   (see *recipe*, page 201)+

Place the butter, sugar, both the flours and the vanilla in
a food processor and process until the dough just comes
together. Divide the dough in half, cover one half with plastic
wrap and set aside in the refrigerator. Roll the remaining half
out between 2 sheets of non-stick baking paper to 4mm thick.
Refrigerate for 30 minutes or until firm.

Preheat oven to 160°C (325°F). Line a large baking tray
with non-stick baking paper. Using various-sized star-shaped
cutters, cut shapes from the rolled-out dough, reserving
any scraps (see *cook's tips*, page 201). Place the stars on the
tray and refrigerate for 10–15 minutes or until firm enough
to handle.

Line a 20cm x 30cm slice tin with non-stick baking paper,
allowing 3cm of paper to sit above the edges. Combine the
dough scraps with the reserved chilled dough and, using the
back of a spoon, press it into the base of the tin. Prick the
base all over with a fork and bake for 20 minutes or until
golden. Allow to cool for 15 minutes.

Spread the jam over the shortbread base and top with
the stars, overlapping them slightly. Bake for 20 minutes or
until the stars are golden. Allow to cool completely in the tin.

Remove the slice from the tin and dust with the extra
sugar to serve. **SERVES 6–8**
+ *You can use ¾ cup (240g) store-bought raspberry jam in
place of the cheat's jam on page 201, if you prefer.*

raspberry and shortbread slice

cheat's raspberry jam

cheat's raspberry jam

2 cups (260g) frozen raspberries
¾ cup (165g) caster (superfine) sugar

Place the raspberries and sugar in a large non-stick frying pan over high heat. Cook, stirring, until the sugar is dissolved. Bring to the boil and cook, stirring continuously, for 8–10 minutes or until the jam has thickened slightly.

Allow the jam to cool completely before spreading onto the shortbread (see *recipe*, page 198), or spoon it into an airtight container immediately. MAKES 1 CUP

Tips: This cheat's jam will keep refrigerated, sealed in an airtight container, for up to 2–3 months. If you like, you can add some extra flavour to the jam – try finely grating in a little lemon rind, or scrape in the seeds of a vanilla bean.

cook's tips

———

○ White rice flour is important in the shortbread recipe – it's what helps to give that classic crisp and crumbly texture to the biscuit when baked.

———

○ When cutting the stars, dip the cookie cutters in a little flour to help prevent the dough from sticking.

———

○ Pressing the dough into the tin with the back of a spoon will give it a smooth, even surface. Bake the base before spreading it with jam to help the shortbread stay crisp beneath the raspberry layer.

———

○ This cheat's jam recipe, using frozen raspberries (no need to even thaw them!), is super simple to make and gives the shortbread slice a lovely tart flavour. With no extra additives – just fruit and sugar – you'll notice plenty of tiny seeds and a vibrant jewel-like colour.

———

○ If you prefer, you can use ¾ cup (240g) of your favourite store-bought jam for the shortbread instead of the cheat's recipe – try cherry or strawberry.

———

○ To save on stress during the Christmas season, why not make the shortbread dough in advance and freeze it? Cover it tightly in plastic wrap and freeze for up to 2 months. Allow it to thaw in the fridge completely before baking.

malt cookies

150g unsalted butter, softened
1 cup (160g) icing (confectioner's) sugar, sifted
1 egg
¼ cup (25g) malted milk powder
1 teaspoon vanilla extract
2½ cups (375g) plain (all-purpose) flour, sifted
1 tablespoon cornflour (cornstarch), sifted
1 teaspoon baking powder

Place the butter and sugar in the bowl of an electric mixer and beat for 5 minutes or until pale and creamy. Add the egg, malt and vanilla and beat for a further 1 minute. Add the flour, cornflour and baking powder and beat until a smooth dough forms. Roll the dough out between 2 sheets of non-stick baking paper to 5mm thick and refrigerate for 30 minutes or until firm.

Preheat oven to 160°C (325°F). Line 2 baking trays with non-stick baking paper. Using various-sized scalloped or fluted cookie cutters[+] lightly dusted in flour, cut shapes from the dough, re-rolling any scraps. Place the cookies on the trays and use a skewer to pierce them with small holes. Bake for 13–15 minutes or until golden. Allow to cool on the trays before serving. MAKES 12[++]

+ Various cookie cutters can be used to make different-shaped cookies. Other kitchen equipment, such as small tart and pie tins, can also be used. For extra decorative flair, use metal or bamboo skewers to make holes and cut-outs.

++ The number of biscuits this recipe makes will depend on the size of the cookie cutters used.

ginger snaps

150g unsalted butter, softened
½ cup (90g) light brown sugar
⅔ cup (230g) golden syrup
1 egg
3 cups (450g) plain (all-purpose) flour, sifted
1 tablespoon cornflour (cornstarch), sifted
1 teaspoon baking powder
½ teaspoon bicarbonate of (baking) soda
1 tablespoon ground ginger

Place the butter, sugar and golden syrup in the bowl of an electric mixer and beat for 5 minutes or until pale and creamy. Add the egg and beat until well combined. Add the flour, cornflour, baking powder, bicarbonate of soda and ginger and beat until a smooth dough forms. Roll the dough out between 2 sheets of non-stick baking paper to 5mm thick and refrigerate for 30 minutes or until firm.

Preheat oven to 180°C (350°F). Line 2 baking trays with non-stick baking paper. Using various-sized scalloped or fluted cookie cutters lightly dusted in flour, cut shapes from the dough, re-rolling any scraps. Place the cookies on the trays and use a skewer to pierce them with small holes. Bake for 8–9 minutes or until golden. Allow to cool on the trays before serving. MAKES 12[+]

+ The number of biscuits this recipe makes will depend on the size of the cookie cutters used.

Tips: The colder the dough, the easier it is to cut out shapes and transfer to baking trays. If your dough does become a little soft, simply refrigerate for 5–10 minutes or until firm again. Once baked, make sure the cookies have cooled completely before storing them in an airtight container. This will ensure they stay crisp and crunchy for up to 4 days.

malt cookies + ginger snaps

chocolate and peppermint creams

chocolate and peppermint creams

150g unsalted butter, softened
½ cup (90g) light brown sugar
½ cup (175g) golden syrup
1½ cups (225g) plain (all-purpose) flour, sifted
¼ cup (25g) cocoa powder, sifted
1 teaspoon bicarbonate of (baking) soda, sifted
200g dark chocolate, chopped
peppermint cream
2½ cups (400g) icing (confectioner's) sugar, sifted
2 tablespoons milk
½ teaspoon peppermint extract

Place the butter, sugar and golden syrup in the bowl of an electric mixer and beat for 8–10 minutes or until pale and creamy. Add the flour, cocoa and bicarbonate of soda and beat until a smooth dough forms. Add the chocolate and mix well to combine. Refrigerate for 30 minutes or until firm.

Preheat oven to 180°C (350°F). Line 2 baking trays with non-stick baking paper. Roll 1-tablespoon portions of the dough into balls. Place on the trays and flatten slightly, allowing room to spread. Bake for 10–12 minutes or until the cookies are just cracked on top. Allow to cool on the trays for 5 minutes. Transfer to wire racks to cool completely.

To make the peppermint cream, place the sugar, milk and peppermint extract in a clean bowl of the electric mixer and beat for 3–4 minutes or until smooth.

Spread the underside of half the biscuits with the peppermint cream and sandwich with the remaining biscuits to serve. MAKES 18
Tip: Filled peppermint creams will keep in an airtight container for up to 1 week. It helps to place non-stick baking paper between the cookies to ensure they don't stick together.

sour cherry and lemon shortbread fingers

120g unsalted butter, softened
1 cup (220g) caster (superfine) sugar
1 egg
1 teaspoon vanilla extract
1¾ cups (260g) plain (all-purpose) flour
1 teaspoon baking powder
1 tablespoon finely grated lemon rind
sour cherry jam
½ cup (100g) dried sour cherries
¼ cup (80g) store-bought strawberry jam
1 tablespoon caster (superfine) sugar

To make the sour cherry jam, place the cherries, jam and sugar in a food processor and process until a rough paste forms. Transfer to a small saucepan over high heat, bring to the boil and cook, stirring, for 2 minutes or until thickened. Remove from the heat and set aside to cool completely.

Place the butter and sugar in the bowl of an electric mixer and beat for 4 minutes or until pale and fluffy. Add the egg and vanilla and beat to combine. Add the flour, baking powder and lemon rind and mix until just combined.

Divide the dough in half and roll each piece out between 2 sheets of non-stick baking paper to make 2 x 16cm x 22cm rectangles. Use a ruler to help you check the rectangles are the correct size and place them on the trays. Freeze for 30 minutes or until firm.

Spread the sour cherry jam over 1 rectangle of dough and top with the remaining rectangle. Wrap in plastic wrap and freeze for a further 1 hour or until very firm.

Preheat oven to 180°C (350°F). Line 2 large baking trays with non-stick baking paper. Remove the plastic wrap and, using a sharp knife, trim and discard the edges from the dough. Using the ruler as a guide, cut the dough into 1cm-thick lengths and place on the trays. Bake for 10–12 minutes or until golden. Allow the shortbread to cool on the trays before serving. MAKES 20
Tip: You can freeze these cookies in an airtight container for up to 3 months. Defrost at room temperature for 20–30 minutes or heat them in a 160°C (325°F) oven for 10 minutes or until warmed through.

sour cherry and lemon shortbread fingers

spiced brown sugar cookies

spiced brown sugar cookies

2 cups (320g) icing (confectioner's) sugar
3 teaspoons ground cinnamon
2¼ cups (335g) plain (all-purpose) flour
½ teaspoon ground ginger
½ teaspoon allspice
¼ teaspoon ground cloves
¼ teaspoon ground nutmeg
¼ teaspoon bicarbonate of (baking) soda
120g unsalted butter, softened
1 cup (175g) light brown sugar
⅓ cup (115g) golden syrup
1 egg
1 teaspoon vanilla extract

Preheat oven to 180°C (350°F). Line 2 large baking trays with non-stick baking paper. Place the icing sugar and 2 teaspoons of the cinnamon in a large bowl. Mix to combine and set aside.

Place the flour and the remaining 1 teaspoon of cinnamon in a medium bowl. Add the ginger, allspice, cloves, nutmeg and bicarbonate of soda. Mix to combine and set aside.

Place the butter, brown sugar and golden syrup in the bowl of an electric mixer and beat for 3 minutes or until pale and fluffy. Add the egg and vanilla and beat to combine. Add the flour mixture and beat until just combined. Roll 1-tablespoon portions of the dough into balls and place on the trays, allowing room to spread. Bake for 8–10 minutes or until golden and slightly cracked. Transfer to wire racks to cool for 10 minutes. Place the biscuits in the spiced sugar and gently toss to coat. Return to the racks and allow to cool completely before serving. MAKES 36

Tip: These cookies will keep in an airtight container for up to 1 week. It helps to place non-stick baking paper between the cookies to ensure they don't stick together.

coconut and jam hearts

125g unsalted butter, chopped
½ cup (110g) caster (superfine) sugar
1 egg
1 teaspoon vanilla extract
1½ cups (225g) plain (all-purpose) flour, sifted
½ teaspoon baking powder, sifted
½ cup (40g) desiccated coconut
icing (confectioner's) sugar, for dusting
½ cup (160g) store-bought raspberry or strawberry jam

Place the butter and sugar in the bowl of an electric mixer and beat for 6 minutes or until pale and creamy. Add the egg and vanilla and beat until well combined. Add the flour, baking powder and coconut and beat for a further 1 minute or until well combined. Refrigerate for 30 minutes or until firm.

Preheat oven to 180°C (350°F). Line 2 large baking trays with non-stick baking paper. Divide the dough in half and roll each portion out between 2 sheets of non-stick baking paper to 3mm thick. Using a 7cm round cookie cutter, cut 24 rounds from the dough. Place on the trays. Using a 4cm heart-shaped cutter, cut and discard heart shapes from the centre of 12 of the rounds+. Bake for 8–10 minutes or until golden. Allow to cool on the trays.

Dust the cut-out rounds with icing sugar. Spread the plain rounds with jam and sandwich with the cut-out rounds. MAKES 12
+ You can bake the little cut-out hearts if you wish – they'll need a bit less time in the oven. They're ready when they're golden.
Tip: These cookies will keep in an airtight container for up to 1 week. It helps to place non-stick baking paper between the cookies to ensure they don't stick together.

coconut and jam hearts

caramel shortbread sandwiches

150g unsalted butter, softened
⅓ cup (55g) icing (confectioner's) sugar, sifted
1 teaspoon vanilla extract
1½ cups (225g) plain (all-purpose) flour, sifted
2 tablespoons cornflour (cornstarch), sifted
⅔ cup (200g) store-bought thick caramel or dulce de leche

Place the butter, sugar and vanilla in the bowl of an electric mixer and beat for 8–10 minutes or until pale and creamy. Add the flour and cornflour and beat until a smooth dough forms. Roll the dough out between 2 sheets of non-stick baking paper to 5mm thick and refrigerate for 30 minutes or until firm.

Preheat oven to 180°C (350°F). Line 2 large baking trays with non-stick baking paper. Using a 4.5cm round cookie cutter, cut 40 rounds from the dough. Place the cookies on the trays. Bake for 10–12 minutes or until just golden. Allow to cool completely on the trays.

Spread half the shortbreads with the caramel and sandwich with the remaining shortbreads. **MAKES 20**

cranberry shortbread hearts

150g unsalted butter, chopped and softened
⅓ cup (55g) icing (confectioner's) sugar, sifted
1 teaspoon vanilla extract
1½ cups (225g) plain (all-purpose) flour, sifted
2 tablespoons cornflour (cornstarch), sifted
¾ cup (100g) sweetened dried cranberries, chopped

Place the butter, sugar and vanilla in the bowl of an electric mixer and beat for 8 minutes or until pale and creamy. Add the flour, cornflour and cranberries and beat until just combined. Roll the mixture out between 2 sheets of non-stick baking paper to 3mm thick. Refrigerate for 30 minutes or until firm.

Preheat oven to 160°C (325°F). Line 2 large baking trays with non-stick baking paper. Using an 8cm heart-shaped cutter, cut 14 hearts from the dough, re-rolling as necessary. Place the hearts on the trays. Using a 3mm round piping nozzle, cut a hole in the top of each cookie.

Bake for 12–14 minutes or until golden. Allow to cool on the trays.

Thread the hearts with ribbon to hang or serve. **MAKES 14**

cranberry and pistachio biscotti

2 cups (300g) plain (all-purpose) flour, sifted
1½ teaspoons baking powder, sifted
¾ cup (165g) caster (superfine) sugar
3 eggs, lightly beaten
2 teaspoons vanilla extract
1 tablespoon finely grated orange rind
1 cup (130g) sweetened dried cranberries
1 cup (140g) shelled unsalted pistachios

Preheat oven to 160°C (325°F). Line 2 large baking trays
with non-stick baking paper. Place the flour, baking powder and
sugar in a large bowl and mix to combine. Add the eggs, vanilla,
orange rind, cranberries and pistachios and mix until a smooth
dough forms. Turn the dough out onto on a well-floured surface
and knead until smooth. Divide in half and roll each piece into
a 20cm log. Flatten slightly and place on the trays. Bake for
30–35 minutes or until firm. Allow to cool. Use a large serrated
knife to slice the logs into 3mm-thick biscotti. Place the
biscotti on the trays and bake for a further 8–10 minutes or
until golden and crisp. Allow to cool on the trays. MAKES 80

lemon and almond cookies

90g unsalted butter, softened
1 cup (220g) raw or Demerara sugar
1 cup (120g) almond meal (ground almonds)
1 cup (150g) plain (all-purpose) flour
½ teaspoon baking powder
2 tablespoons finely grated lemon rind, plus ¼ cup (60ml) juice
1 teaspoon vanilla extract
icing (confectioner's) sugar, for dusting

Place the butter and sugar in the bowl of an electric mixer and
beat for 5 minutes or until pale. Add the almond meal, flour,
baking powder, lemon rind, juice and vanilla. Beat for 2 minutes
or until a dough forms. Roll out between 2 sheets of non-stick
baking paper to 5mm thick and refrigerate for 30 minutes.
    Preheat oven to 160°C (325°F). Line 2 baking trays with
non-stick baking paper. Using an 8.5cm round fluted cutter,
cut 12 rounds from the dough. Using a 3.5cm round cutter,
cut and discard the centre from each cookie. Place on the
trays and bake for 10–12 minutes or until golden. Allow to
cool on the trays. Dust with icing sugar to serve. MAKES 12

gingerbread houses

gingerbread houses

1.2kg plain (all-purpose) flour

2 teaspoons bicarbonate of (baking) soda

1½ cups (260g) light brown sugar

1 tablespoon ground ginger

380g unsalted butter, melted

1⅔ cups (580g) golden syrup

icing (confectioner's) sugar, for dusting

icing

4 cups (640g) icing (confectioner's) sugar

3 eggwhites

¼ teaspoon cream of tartar

1 tablespoon lemon juice

Preheat oven to 180°C (350°F). Place half of each of the flour, bicarbonate of soda, brown sugar and ginger in a large food processor and pulse until combined. Add half the butter and half the golden syrup and process until a dough comes together. Transfer to a large bowl. Repeat with the remaining dry and wet ingredients. Add the second batch of dough to the first and knead until smooth and combined.

Divide the dough into 4 equal pieces. Using your fingers, press each piece into a 25cm x 37cm Swiss roll tin to make 4 rectangles, smoothing the tops with the back of a metal spoon. Bake in 2 batches for 12–15 minutes or until golden.

Download, print and use scissors to cut out the templates at *donnahay.com.au/files/Gingerbread_Houses_large_and_small.pdf*.

Transfer 1 gingerbread sheet onto a large chopping board and begin cutting out the shapes while still hot. Starting with a large house, place the roof template and the templates for the front and back of the house on the gingerbread and, using a metal ruler and sharp knife, cut the shapes+. Cut the roof tile in half where marked and cut out a door on the front of the house. Cut 2 even triangles from the top of the rectangles, lining up with the dotted line to create the rooftop.

Transfer a second gingerbread sheet to a large chopping board. Place the templates for the walls and chimney of the large house on the gingerbread, as well as all the templates for one small house. Cut out the shapes+, ensuring you cut the roof tiles in half, the large and small house walls in half and the chimney in half, where marked. Cut 2 even triangles from the top of the rectangles, lining up with the dotted lines, to create the rooftops. Set aside to cool completely.

Repeat the process with the remaining gingerbread sheets, creating the pieces for the second large house and second small house, leaving out the chimney template in the second batch. Set aside to cool completely.

To make the icing, place the sugar, eggwhites and cream of tartar in the bowl of an electric mixer and beat on high speed for 4–5 minutes or until light and fluffy. Add the lemon juice and beat for a further 2 minutes or until well combined. Place half the icing in a piping bag fitted with a 4mm round nozzle and the remaining icing in a piping bag fitted with a 2mm round nozzle.

Starting with the roof tiles, use the 2mm nozzle to pipe a cross-hatch pattern on the large roofs and a scallop pattern on the small roofs+. Pipe 1 curved window and 4 smaller windows on each of the 2 large house fronts, and 2 windows on the 2 small house fronts. Pipe around each doorway and pipe the doorknobs.

Using the 4mm nozzle, pipe along the 2 long inside edges of the front of the large house and secure the 2 side walls. Leave for 2 minutes or until set. Repeat with the back section of the house. Pipe along the edges of the rooftops and secure the roof tiles to the house, holding for a few minutes until the icing starts to set. Pipe along the top edge of the roof and outline of the house. For the chimney, mark a diagonal line along the rectangles to match the angle of the roof and, using a small serrated knife, cut off both pieces. Pipe along 1 side and stick the 2 pieces together. Pipe on the diagonal edge and press onto the roof. Hold for 2 minutes or until the icing starts to set. Repeat with the remaining pieces to build the remaining houses. Allow to set completely for 20 minutes. Gently push the doors open and dust the roofs with icing sugar. **MAKES 2 LARGE HOUSES AND 2 SMALL HOUSES** + *See the images on page 214 to guide you.*

cook's tips

○ Using scissors, cut out the paper templates along the solid black lines then place them directly on the gingerbread. Use them as stencils, cutting around the outside with a large serrated knife.

○ It's easiest to cut out the shapes while the gingerbread is still warm. While you are working with 1 sheet, set the others aside under a tea towel.

○ Use a metal ruler to help you cut out the door and the top of the roof sections.

○ For a more manageable village, you can halve this recipe to make 1 small house and 1 large house.

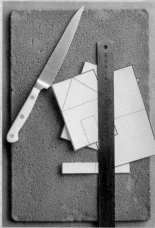

position the templates

the pieces from sheet one

the pieces from sheet two

decorate with a 2mm nozzle

join with the 4mm nozzle

press and hold to secure

○ Use our visuals to
guide you through the
icing and decorating.

salted chocolate gingerbread men

basic gingerbread cookie dough

125g unsalted butter, softened
½ cup (90g) light brown sugar
⅔ cup (230g) golden syrup
2½ cups (375g) plain (all-purpose) flour, sifted
1 teaspoon bicarbonate of (baking) soda, sifted
2 teaspoons ground ginger
1 teaspoon mixed spice

Place the butter and sugar in the bowl of an electric mixer and beat for 10–12 minutes or until pale and creamy. Scrape down the sides of the bowl, add the golden syrup, flour, bicarbonate of soda, ginger and mixed spice. Beat until a smooth dough forms. MAKES 1 QUANTITY
Tips: See the recipes that follow for how to roll out, cut and bake various gingerbread treats. If the dough feels too soft at any stage, you can refrigerate it for a few minutes before continuing. Freeze any leftover dough, wrapped in plastic wrap, for up to 2 months.

chocolate gingerbread cookie dough

125g unsalted butter, chopped and softened
½ cup (90g) light brown sugar
⅔ cup (230g) golden syrup
2⅓ cups (350g) plain (all-purpose) flour, sifted
⅓ cup (35g) cocoa powder, sifted
1 teaspoon bicarbonate of (baking) soda, sifted
2 teaspoons ground ginger
1 teaspoon mixed spice

Place the butter and sugar in the bowl of an electric mixer and beat for 10–12 minutes or until pale and creamy. Scrape down the sides of the bowl and add the golden syrup, flour, cocoa, bicarbonate of soda, ginger and mixed spice. Beat until a smooth dough forms (see *tips*, above). MAKES 1 QUANTITY

basic vanilla snap cookie dough

125g unsalted butter, softened
½ cup (110g) caster (superfine) sugar
1 egg
2 teaspoons vanilla extract
1½ cups (225g) plain (all-purpose) flour, sifted

Place the butter and sugar in the bowl of an electric mixer and beat for 6–8 minutes or until pale and creamy. Add the egg and vanilla and beat for a further 2–3 minutes or until well combined. Add the flour and beat until the mixture just comes together to form a smooth dough. MAKES 1 QUANTITY
Tip: See the recipes that follow for how to roll out, cut and bake various vanilla snap cookies.

salted chocolate gingerbread men

1 x quantity chocolate gingerbread dough (see *recipe*, left)
200g dark chocolate, chopped
3 teaspoons vegetable oil
sea salt flakes, for sprinkling

Divide the dough in half and roll each piece out between 2 sheets of non-stick baking paper to 4mm thick. Refrigerate for 30 minutes or until firm.
Preheat oven to 160°C (325°F). Line 2 large baking trays with non-stick baking paper. Using an 8cm gingerbread-man shaped cutter, cut 20 shapes from the dough, re-rolling as necessary. Place on the trays and bake for 8–10 minutes or until golden. Allow to cool completely on the trays.
Place the chocolate and oil in a heatproof bowl over a saucepan of simmering water and stir until melted and smooth. Dip the bottom half of each biscuit into the chocolate and sprinkle the feet with salt. Return to the trays and refrigerate until set, before serving. MAKES 20
Tips: Cookie cutters in various shapes and sizes are available at homewares retailers, cake-decorating stores and online. Keep these gingerbread men refrigerated until ready to serve. You can use any leftover dough to make more biscuits.

mixed gingerbread christmas trees

1 x quantity basic gingerbread dough (see *recipe*, page 217)
1 x quantity chocolate gingerbread dough (see *recipe*, page 217)
chocolate icing
2 cups (320g) icing (confectioner's) sugar, sifted
¼ cup (25g) cocoa powder, sifted
2 tablespoons boiling water, plus 1 tablespoon extra

Roll each dough out between 2 sheets of non-stick baking
paper to 5mm thick. Refrigerate for 30 minutes or until firm.

Preheat oven to 140°C (275°F). Line 2 large baking trays
with non-stick baking paper. Download, print and use scissors
to cut out the templates at *donnahay.com.au/files/Gingerbread_
Christmas_Trees.pdf*. Alternatively, create your own templates
using the measurements below[+].

Using the templates as a guide and a small sharp knife, cut
the panels for 1 small, 1 medium and 1 large tree from each
sheet of dough, re-rolling as necessary. Using a 2cm and 3cm
star-shaped cutter, cut 6 stars from the dough of your choice.

Place the trees and stars on the trays and bake for
23–25 minutes or until golden and dry to the touch. Allow
to cool completely on the trays.

To make the chocolate icing, place the sugar and cocoa
in a medium bowl. Gradually add the water and whisk until
the mixture is smooth and pliable, only adding the extra
water if necessary.

Spoon the icing into a piping bag fitted with a 5mm round
nozzle. Trim to straighten the edges of the trees, using a
small serrated knife, and pipe icing onto each long edge.
Assemble 3 matching sides together, pressing gently to
attach, and allow to stand for 30 minutes or until set.

Pipe a little icing onto the top of each tree and attach
the stars to serve. MAKES 6

*+ Print the templates from donnahay.com, or use a ruler and
pencil to create your own. Draw 1 panel of each-sized tree on
paper. A small tree is 17cm tall and has an 8cm-wide base. A
medium tree is 22cm tall and has a 9cm-wide base. A large tree
is 29cm tall and has a 10cm-wide base. Use scissors to cut out
the 3 templates. Use the templates to cut 3 panels for each
tree from each sheet of dough.*

gingerbread snowmen

1 x quantity basic gingerbread dough (see *recipe*, page 217)

Roll the dough out between 2 sheets of non-stick baking
paper to 4mm thick. Refrigerate for 30 minutes or until firm.

Preheat oven to 160°C (325°F). Line a baking tray with
non-stick baking paper. Using 10cm and 9cm snowman-shaped
cutters, cut 20 shapes from the dough. Place on the tray
and bake for 10–12 minutes or until golden. Allow to cool
on the tray, before serving. MAKES 20

gingerbread antlers

1 x quantity basic gingerbread dough (see *recipe*, page 217)

Roll the dough out between 2 sheets of non-stick baking
paper to 4mm thick. Refrigerate for 30 minutes or until firm.

Preheat oven to 160°C (325°F). Line a baking tray with
non-stick baking paper. Using an 11cm antler-shaped cutter,
cut 14 shapes from the dough. Place on the tray and bake
for 10–12 minutes or until golden. Allow to cool on the tray,
before serving. MAKES 14

mixed gingerbread christmas trees

gingerbread christmas cookie garlands

1 x quantity basic gingerbread dough (see *recipe*, page 217)
1 x quantity chocolate gingerbread dough (see *recipe*, page 217)

Roll each dough out between 2 sheets of non-stick baking paper to 5mm thick. Refrigerate for 30 minutes or until firm.

Preheat oven to 140°C (275°F). Line 2 large baking trays with non-stick baking paper. Using various-shaped 5cm cutters, cut a selection of gingerbread men, Christmas trees, stars and snowmen, re-rolling the dough as necessary. Use a 6mm round piping nozzle to cut 2 holes in the centre of each shape. Place on the trays and bake for 20–22 minutes or until golden and dry to the touch. Allow to cool completely on the trays.

Thread half the cookies onto a length of ribbon and tie the ends to secure. Repeat with the remaining cookies+. **MAKES 2**
+ *This recipe is designed to make 2 x 32-cookie garlands.*
Tips: You can store the gingerbread cookies in an airtight container for up to 1–2 weeks. Hang them on Christmas Eve. Cookie cutters in various shapes and sizes are available to buy from homewares retailers, cake-decorating stores and online.

gingerbread men wreaths

1 x quantity basic gingerbread dough (see *recipe*, page 217)

Roll the dough out between 2 sheets of non-stick baking paper to 5mm thick. Refrigerate for 30 minutes or until firm.

Preheat oven to 140°C (275°F). Line 2 large baking trays with non-stick baking paper. Using a 7cm gingerbread-man shaped cutter, cut 22 shapes from the dough, re-rolling as necessary. Arrange on the trays to form 2 rings, with alternate hands and feet overlapping. Bake for 30 minutes or until golden and dry to the touch. Allow to cool completely on the trays.

Thread lengths of ribbon through the gingerbread men, leaving enough excess to hang the wreaths. **MAKES 2**
Tip: You can store the gingerbread wreaths in an airtight container for up to 1–2 weeks. Hang them on Christmas Eve.

gingerbread advent calendar stars

1 x quantity basic gingerbread dough (see *recipe*, page 217)
1½ cups (240g) icing (confectioner's) sugar, sifted
1 eggwhite

Roll the dough out between 2 sheets of non-stick baking
paper to 5mm thick. Refrigerate for 30 minutes or until firm.
    Preheat oven to 140°C (275°F). Line 2 large baking trays
with non-stick baking paper. Using star-shaped cutters, cut
8 x 5.5cm stars, 8 x 6.5cm stars, 4 x 7.5cm stars and 5 x 9.5cm
stars from the dough+. Use the tip of a 6mm round piping
nozzle to cut a hole in the top of each star. Place the stars
on the trays and bake for 18–20 minutes or until golden
and dry to the touch. Allow to cool completely on the trays.
    Place the sugar and eggwhite in a medium bowl and mix
to combine. Spoon into a piping bag fitted with a 2mm round
nozzle. Pipe borders on the stars. Number them from 1 to 25.
Allow to set and thread onto ribbon or string to hang. MAKES 25
+ *There's enough gingerbread dough to make 40 cookies. Freeze
the leftover dough or cut and bake extra gingerbread cookies.*

gingerbread buttons

1 x quantity basic gingerbread dough (see *recipe*, page 217)

Roll the dough out between 2 sheets of non-stick baking
paper to 5mm thick. Refrigerate for 30 minutes or until firm.
    Preheat oven to 140°C (275°F). Line 2 large baking trays
with non-stick baking paper. Using a 5cm cookie cutter, cut
32 rounds from the dough, re-rolling as necessary. Using a
3cm round cutter, indent to mark a border on each round.
Using the tip of a 6mm round piping nozzle, cut 2 holes
from the centre of each cookie. Place on the trays and bake
for 18–20 minutes or until golden and dry to the touch.
Allow to cool completely on the trays. Thread the cookies
onto ribbon and use as decorations or napkin rings. MAKES 32
*Tips: Extra cookies will keep in an airtight container for up to
1–2 weeks. You could also use the chocolate gingerbread cookie
dough (see recipe, page 217) to make these buttons, if you prefer.*

gingerbread heart garlands

1 x quantity basic gingerbread dough (see *recipe*, page 217)

Roll the dough out between 2 sheets of non-stick baking paper to 5mm thick. Refrigerate for 30 minutes or until firm.
  Preheat oven to 160°C (325°F). Line 2 large baking trays with non-stick baking paper. Using a 3.5cm heart-shaped cutter, cut 80 hearts from the dough, re-rolling as necessary. Using the tip of a 3mm round piping nozzle, cut a hole in the top of each heart. Place on the trays and bake for 12–15 minutes or until golden and dry to the touch. Allow to cool completely on the trays. Thread onto string or ribbon to hang[+]. **MAKES 8**
[+] *This recipe is designed to make 8 x 10-cookie garlands, but you can choose to hang them whichever way you like.*

lemon and vanilla snowflakes

1 x quantity basic vanilla snap dough (see *recipe*, page 217)
1 tablespoon finely grated lemon rind
1 cup (160g) icing (confectioner's) sugar, sifted
1 tablespoon boiling water

Follow the dough recipe, adding the lemon rind with the egg.
  Roll the dough out between 2 sheets of non-stick baking paper to 3mm thick. Refrigerate for 30 minutes or until firm.
  Preheat oven to 140°C (275°F). Line 2 large baking trays with non-stick baking paper. Using assorted snowflake-shaped cutters, cut 25 shapes from the dough, re-rolling as necessary. Using the tip of a 2mm round piping nozzle, cut a hole in the top of each snowflake. Place on the trays and bake for 8–10 minutes or until golden. Allow to cool completely on the trays.
  Place the sugar and water in a small bowl and mix until smooth. Spoon into a piping bag fitted with a 2mm round nozzle and pipe onto snowflakes to decorate. Allow to set before threading with string or ribbon to hang. **MAKES 25**

chocolate-chip gingerbread cookies

100g dark chocolate, chopped
1 x quantity basic gingerbread dough (see *recipe*, page 217)

Preheat oven to 160°C (325°F). Line 2 large baking trays with non-stick baking paper. Add the chocolate to the dough and gently mix to combine. Roll 1-tablespoon portions of the mixture into balls and place on the trays, allowing room to spread. Flatten slightly and bake for 10–12 minutes or until golden. Allow to cool completely on the trays, before serving. **MAKES 24**
Tip: Paired with a glass of milk, these cookies make the perfect treat to leave out for Santa on Christmas Eve. You can bake them ahead of time and keep in an airtight container for 1–2 weeks.

vanilla star wreaths

1 x quantity basic vanilla snap dough (see *recipe*, page 217)
icing (confectioner's) sugar, for dusting

Roll the dough out between 2 sheets of non-stick baking paper to 3mm thick. Refrigerate for 30 minutes or until firm.

Preheat oven to 140°C (275°F). Line 2 large baking trays with non-stick baking paper. Trace 2 x 14cm circles onto each sheet and turn the paper over to prevent any pencil marks transferring.

Using an 8cm star-shaped cutter, cut 28 stars from the dough, re-rolling as necessary. Arrange 7 stars around each circle, overlapping the tips to create wreath shapes. Bake for 20–25 minutes or until golden. Allow to cool completely on the trays.

Dust with icing sugar and tie the wreaths with string or ribbon to hang. **MAKES 4**
Tip: Store wreaths in an airtight container for up to 2–3 days and hang them on Christmas Eve.

gingerbread reindeer

1 x quantity basic gingerbread dough (see *recipe*, page 217)

Roll the dough out between 2 sheets of non-stick baking paper to 4mm thick. Refrigerate for 30 minutes or until firm.

Preheat oven to 160°C (325°F). Line a baking tray with non-stick baking paper. Using 7cm and 5cm deer-shaped cutters, cut 32 shapes from the dough. Place on the tray and bake for 8–10 minutes or until golden. Allow to cool on the trays, before serving. **MAKES 32**

spiced vanilla reindeer

1 x quantity basic vanilla snap dough (see *recipe*, page 217)
1 teaspoon ground cinnamon
1 teaspoon mixed spice
icing
½ cup (80g) icing (confectioner's) sugar, sifted
2 teaspoons boiling water

Follow the dough recipe, adding the cinnamon and mixed spice with the flour. Roll the dough out between 2 sheets of non-stick baking paper to 5mm thick and refrigerate for 30 minutes or until firm.

Preheat oven to 160°C (325°F). Line 2 large baking trays with non-stick baking paper. Using a 7cm deer-shaped cutter, cut 32 shapes from the dough, re-rolling as necessary. Place on the trays and bake for 8–10 minutes or until golden. Allow to cool completely on the trays.

To make the icing, place the sugar and water in a small bowl and mix until smooth.

Spoon into a piping bag fitted with a 2mm round nozzle and pipe a nose and three tail spots on each deer to decorate. Allow to set before serving. **MAKES 32**

chocolate cookie christmas tree

1 x quantity basic vanilla snap dough (see *recipe*, page 217)
¼ cup (25g) cocoa powder, sifted
icing (confectioner's) sugar, for dusting
icing
½ cup (80g) icing (confectioner's) sugar, sifted
2 teaspoons boiling water

Follow the dough recipe, adding the cocoa with the flour. Roll the dough out between 2 sheets of non-stick baking paper to 3mm thick. Refrigerate for 30 minutes or until firm.

Preheat oven to 160°C (325°F). Line 2 large baking trays with non-stick baking paper. Use 12cm, 11cm, 10cm, 9cm, 8cm, 7cm, 6cm, 5cm, 4cm and 3cm six-pointed star-shaped cutters to cut 3 stars of each size from the dough, re-rolling as necessary. Place on the trays and bake for 10 minutes or until dry to the touch. Allow to cool on the trays for 5 minutes. Transfer to wire racks to cool completely.

To make the icing, place the sugar and water in a small bowl and mix until smooth.

Stack the stars from largest to smallest on a serving plate, securing each star with a little of the icing. Dust the tree with icing sugar to serve. **MAKES 1**

Tip: Cookie cutters in various shapes and sizes are available to buy from homewares retailers, cake-decorating stores and online.

spiced vanilla reindeer + chocolate cookie christmas tree

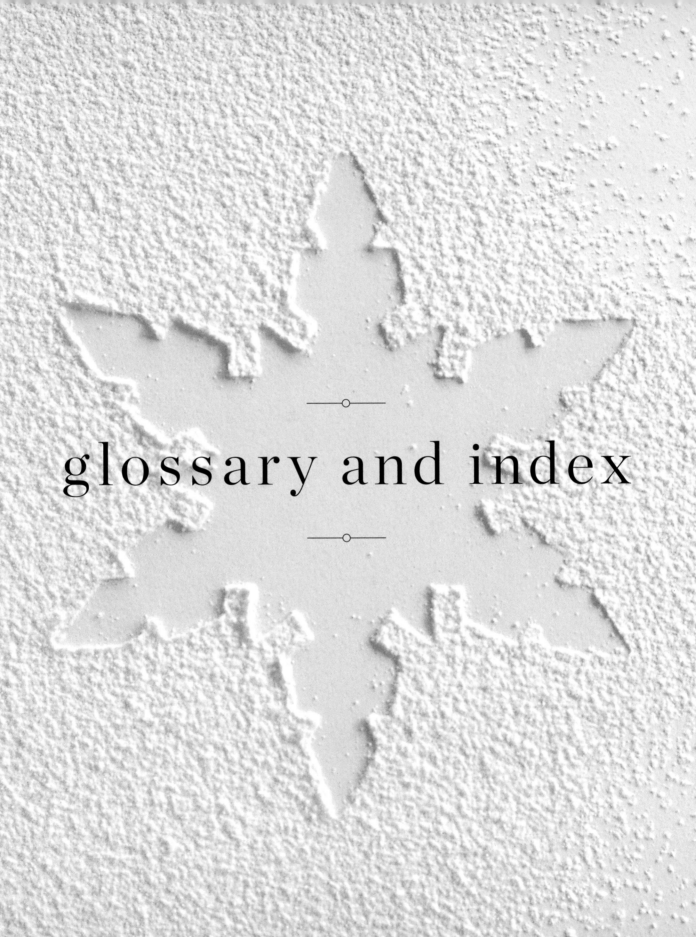

glossary and index

In the glossary, you'll find basic information on pantry staples, plus notes on any of the unusual ingredients called for in this book. There are also some really useful pages of global measures, temperatures, weights and common conversions. Find all recipes listed alphabetically by name in the index, as well as grouped by their main ingredients.

amaretti biscuits

Amaretti biscuits, or macarons, are traditional Italian almond-flavoured biscuits. Made with sugar, eggwhites and almonds, they're light, crisp and often have a slightly chewy centre. Find them in supermarkets, Italian grocers and delicatessens.

arborio rice

This white rice, with a short plump grain, cooks to a soft texture while retaining a firm interior. It has surface starch that creates a creaminess in risottos when cooked to al dente. Find it in supermarkets.

baking powder

A raising agent used in baking, consisting of bicarbonate of soda and/or cream of tartar. Most are gluten free (check the labels). Baking powder that is kept beyond its use-by date can often lose effectiveness. To create a makeshift self-raising (self-rising) flour, add 2 teaspoons of baking powder to each 1 cup (150g) of plain (all-purpose) flour and sift repeatedly to combine.

bay leaves

These aromatic leaves of the bay tree are available both fresh from some greengrocers and dried from the spice section of supermarkets. Add to soups, stews and stocks for a savoury depth of flavour. Remove before serving.

bicarbonate of (baking) soda

Also known as baking soda, bicarbonate of soda (sodium bicarbonate) is an alkaline powder used to help leaven baked goods and neutralise acids. It's also often hailed as having multiple uses around the home, notably as an effective cleaner.

black sea salt flakes

Naturally coloured with carbon or charcoal, black sea salt flakes are interchangeable with regular sea salt flakes. Find them at specialty grocers and most supermarkets.

blue swimmer crab

A common edible crab named for its vibrant blue-coloured shell. Available green (raw) and cooked from fish shops and markets. Ask your fishmonger to cut and clean the crab if necessary, and eat on the day of purchase.

breadcrumbs

To make breadcrumbs, cut and discard the crusts from 2 slices (140g) stale white or sourdough bread. Tear the bread into pieces and place in a food processor. Pulse into either coarse or fine crumbs. **MAKES 1 CUP**

brioche slider buns

Soft and light with a glossy exterior, these small French-style brioche rolls are perfect for making mini burgers or lobster rolls. Find them at bakeries, greengrocers and most supermarkets.

broccolini (tenderstem)

Also known as tenderstem broccoli, broccolini is a cross between gai lan (Chinese broccoli) and broccoli. Sold in bunches, it can be substituted for regular heads of broccoli.

butter

Unless stated otherwise in a recipe, butter should be at room temperature for cooking. It should not be half-melted or too soft to handle. We use unsalted butter in most recipes but you can use regular salted butter if you prefer.

buttermilk

Once a by-product of the butter churning process, commercial buttermilk is created by adding a bacteria to skimmed milk. Its acidity and tangy creaminess is often harnessed to make fluffy pancakes, moist cakes, light scones and rich dressings. It's sold in cartons in the refrigerated section of supermarkets.

cheese

cream

A fresh, salted, spreadable cheese sold in tubs or foil-wrapped blocks. Mostly used as a spread for sandwiches and bagels or as the base for cream cheese frosting that tops carrot cakes and muffins.

gruyère

A firm cow's milk cheese with a smooth ivory interior and a natural brushed rind. Popular in Switzerland as a table cheese and cooked into fondues, gratins and quiches. It makes a fabulous melting cheese, especially in toasted sandwiches.

mascarpone

A fresh Italian triple-cream curd-style cheese, mascarpone has a smooth consistency, similar to thick (double) cream. Available in tubs from delis and most supermarkets, it's used in sauces and desserts such as tiramisu, as well as in icings and frostings for its luscious creaminess and subtle tang.

pecorino

A popular hard Italian cheese made from sheep's milk, pecorino has a sharp flavour similar to that of parmesan cheese. Available at delicatessens, cheese shops and most supermarkets. If unavailable, substitute with parmesan.

ricotta

A creamy, finely grained white cheese, ricotta means 'recooked' in Italian, a reference to the way the cheese is produced by heating the whey left over from making other cheeses. Fresh full-cream and low-fat ricotta is available at the deli counter of supermarkets. Choose fresh full-cream ricotta for most recipes, especially gnocchi, cheesecakes and pancakes – don't substitute with the smoother variety that's pre-packaged in tubs.

chickpeas (garbanzo beans)

If not ground into besan flour, these legumes are used whole in soups and stews or blended into hummus. Dried chickpeas must be soaked before cooking, while canned chickpeas can just be rinsed and drained.

chocolate

dark

Rich and semi-sweet, regular dark chocolate usually contains 45–55% cocoa solids. It's sold in blocks and is ideal for use in baking. Dark chocolate that has 70% cocoa solids is labelled as such, and has a more bitter, intense flavour with a slightly powdery texture.

melted

To melt chocolate, place the required amount of chopped chocolate in a heatproof bowl over a saucepan of simmering water (the bowl shouldn't touch the water). Stir until smooth.

milk

Sweet and smooth, with a paler colour than dark chocolate, milk chocolate is the most popular for eating. It usually contains around 25% cocoa solids.

white

Made from cocoa butter and milk solids, white chocolate is super sweet and creamy in colour.

coconut

desiccated

The flesh of coconuts which has been shredded and dried, desiccated coconut is unsweetened and quite powdery.

flakes

Coconut flakes are large and thin and have been shaved from coconut flesh and dried. Sweet with a chewy texture, they're used for decorating cakes and in baking or muesli. You can toast them in the oven until golden.

shredded

Coarser than desiccated coconut, shredded coconut is perfect for adding texture to slices and cookies.

coriander (cilantro)

This aromatic green herb is also called cilantro. The delicate leaves have a signature flavour and, sometimes along with the finely chopped roots and stems, are commonly used in Asian and Mexican cooking.

coriander seeds

These dried seeds of the coriander plant are an Indian staple. They're sold ground or whole and are one of the base ingredients in curry. They're different to (and cannot be substituted with) the fresh leaves.

cream

The fat content of these different varieties of creams determines their names and uses.

crème fraîche

A rich, tangy, fermented cream, traditionally from France, crème fraîche has a minimum fat content of 35%. It's available at grocers, delicatessens and most supermarkets.

double (thick)

Often called heavy, or dollop, cream, double cream has a butter fat content of 40–50%. It's usually served as a side with warm puddings, pies and rich cakes.

single (pouring)

With a butter fat content of 20–30%, this thin cream is the variety most commonly used in savoury cooking, and for making desserts like ice-cream, panna cotta and custard. It can be whipped to a light and airy consistency. It's also called pure or whipping cream.

sour

A fermented cream with a minimum fat content of 35%, sour cream is readily available in supermarkets and used for its creamy-yet-tangy flavour.

crystallised ginger

Crystallised ginger gives cookies and slices a warm spicy flavour with a sweet finish. The firm, dried ginger pieces, coated in sugar, are available in supermarkets and health food stores.

cumin seeds

This ancient spice, from a plant of the parsley family, is common in Middle-Eastern and Indian cooking. The small long brown seeds are peppery and aromatic with distinct flavour, particularly when toasted. Buy cumin seeds, whole or ground, from the spice section of supermarkets.

dill

A flavourful herb with feathery fronds, dill is used mostly fresh in salads, dips or as a garnish for smoked salmon or trout canapés. Both the fronds and seeds are used in the pickling of cucumbers and give dill pickles their signature flavour. If cooking with dill, add it in the last moments – heat can reduce its intensity.

dulce de leche

This thick milk caramel, common in Latin American desserts, is made by slowly heating and thickening sweetened milk. You can buy it ready-made in jars from supermarkets and grocers. Make your own by gently boiling an unopened can (not a ring-pull can) of sweetened condensed milk for 2–3 hours. The longer it's cooked, the thicker, darker and more intense the caramel flavour becomes. Dulce de leche can be used as a filling for tarts, as a topping on cakes or simply drizzled over ice-cream.

eggs

The standard egg size used in this book is 60g. It is important to use the right-sized eggs for a recipe, as this will affect the outcome of baked goods. The correct volume is especially important when using eggwhites to make meringues. You should use eggs at room temperature for baking.

eschalots (french shallots)

A member of the onion family, eschalots are smaller and have a milder flavour than brown, red or white onions. Used frequently in European cooking, they look like small elongated brown onions with purple and beige skins – not to be confused with green or spring onions.

fennel seeds

The green seeds of the common fennel plant impart a warm anise note to breads and chutneys as well as fish, meat and vegetable dishes. Toast and/or grind them for maximum flavour.

flour

00 (superfine)

Graded '00' for its texture via the Italian milling system, this superfine flour makes for soft and stretchy dough and is used for making pizza and pasta. It's available from the baking aisle of most supermarkets.

cornflour (cornstarch)

When made from ground corn or maize, cornflour is gluten free. It's quite often blended with water or stock to be used as a thickening agent. Not to be confused with cornflour in the United States, which is finely ground corn meal.

plain (all-purpose)

Ground from the endosperm of wheat, plain white flour contains no raising agent.

rice

Rice flour is a fine flour made from ground rice. Available in white and brown varieties, it's often used as a thickening agent in baking, in cookies and shortbreads, and to coat foods when cooking Asian dishes like crispy tofu or tempura.

self-raising (self-rising)

Ground from the endosperm of wheat, self-raising flour contains raising agents including sodium carbonates and calcium phosphates. To make it using plain flour, add 2 teaspoons of baking powder to every 1 cup (150g) of flour.

spelt

Milled from the ancient cereal grain, spelt flour boasts more nutrients and is better tolerated by some than regular flour. White spelt flour is easier to bake with, while wholemeal has more of the grain's goodness. It lends a warm, nutty flavour to breads and cakes. Find spelt flour in the health aisle of supermarkets.

wholemeal (whole-wheat)

Ground from the whole grain of wheat and thus keeping more of its nutrients and fibre, this flour is available in plain (all-purpose) and self-raising (self-rising) varieties from most supermarkets and health food stores. Aside from its nutritional value, it gives pasta, breads, cakes and other baked goods a unique body and flavour.

ginger nut biscuits

A popular, commercially made sweet biscuit flavoured with ground ginger and spices. Often called for in baking recipes to be crushed and pressed into bases for slices and cheesecakes. Similar but different to ginger snap biscuits, ginger nuts are very hard in texture. For the recipes in this book, you need the super crunchy hard (not chewy) variety. Sold in packs at major supermarkets.

horseradish

A pungent root vegetable that releases mustard oil when cut or grated, horseradish oxidises quickly, so use it immediately after cutting or cover with water or vinegar. Fresh horseradish is delicious grated over beef or into mashed potato – find it at greengrocers. You can also buy it ready-grated or as horseradish cream in jars from the supermarket.

juniper berries

The aromatic and bitter dried berries of a hardy evergreen bush, juniper is used for pickling vegetables, flavouring sauces and, most famously, for infusing gin.

light corn syrup

Find light corn syrup at specialty food stores and baking retailers. It serves many purposes – from controlling sugar crystallisation in candy to thickening and balancing the flavour in jams.

liquid glucose

Liquid glucose is used in the making of confectionery such as hard candy, marshmallow and jellies. Find it in the baking aisle of supermarkets.

maple syrup

A sweetener made from the sap of the maple tree. Be sure to use pure maple syrup rather than imitation or maple-flavoured pancake syrup.

marjoram

A delicately flavoured herb, related to mint and very similar in flavour to oregano.

micro herbs

The baby version of fresh herbs, these tiny edible leaves have a great intensity of flavour despite their size. They make a beautiful garnish – sprinkle them liberally over cooked dishes or into salads, or place them onto individual canapés. Find them in small pots and in a loose mix at farmers' markets and greengrocers.

mirin (japanese rice wine)

A pale yellow Japanese cooking wine made from glutinous rice and alcohol. Sweet mirin is flavoured with corn syrup.

mustard

dijon

Also called French mustard, this creamy, mild-flavoured condiment originated in France. It's an important ingredient in vinaigrette.

hot english

Pungent and yellow in colour with an intense heat, pair English mustard with ham or roast beef.

oil

olive

Olive oil is graded according to its flavour, aroma and acidity. Extra virgin is the highest quality olive oil – it contains no more than 1% acid. Virgin is the next best – it contains 1.5% or less acid. Bottles labelled simply 'olive oil' contain a blend of refined and unrefined virgin olive oil. 'Light' olive oil is the least pure in quality and shouldn't be confused with light-flavoured extra virgin olive oil. Where possible, it's best to keep a bottle of extra virgin olive oil on-hand for everyday use in cooking and dressings, plus a light-flavoured extra virgin olive oil for baking.

sesame

Pressed from sesame seeds, sesame oil is used in Asian cuisine more as a nutty, full-flavoured seasoning than a cooking medium.

vegetable

Oils sourced from plants or seeds, such as sunflower or grapeseed oil, with very mild, unobtrusive flavours. Often called for in baking recipes, like muffins or loaf cakes. It's handy to keep a bottle of all-purpose oil labelled simply 'vegetable oil' on-hand in your pantry.

pancetta

Cured and rolled Italian-style pork that is like prosciutto but less salty and with a softer texture. It's sold in flat pieces or chunks, or is thinly sliced into rounds.

paprika

smoked

Unlike Hungarian paprika, the Spanish style known as pimentón is deep and smoky in flavour. It is made from smoked, ground pimento peppers and comes in varying intensities from sweet and mild (dulce), bittersweet medium hot (agridulce) to hot (picante).

sweet

Made from dried, ground red capsicums (peppers), this earthy coloured powder is used as a spice, seasoning and garnish.

pastry

Make your own or use one of the many store-bought varieties, which are sold frozen in blocks or ready-rolled into sheets. Defrost in the fridge before use.

filo (phyllo)

Extremely thin sheets of pastry, popular in Turkish, Greek and Middle-Eastern baking. Each sheet is usually brushed with oil or melted butter and then layered, before encasing a filling. Keep sheets from drying out while working by covering with a clean damp tea towel.

puff and butter puff

This pastry is quite difficult to make, so many cooks opt to use store-bought puff pastry. It can be bought in blocks from patisseries, or is sold in both block and sheet forms in supermarkets. Butter puff pastry is light and flaky, perfect for sweet pies and tarts.

shortcrust
Shortcrust pastry is a savoury or sweet pastry that is available ready-made in blocks and frozen sheets. Keep a supply in the freezer for last-minute pies, or make your own:

1½ cups (225g) plain (all-purpose) flour
125g cold unsalted butter, chopped
3 egg yolks
1 tablespoon iced water

Place the flour and butter in a food processor and process in short bursts until the mixture resembles fine breadcrumbs. While the motor is running, add the egg yolks and water. Process until a dough just comes together. Turn out the dough onto a lightly floured surface and gently bring together to form a ball. Flatten the dough into a disc, wrap in plastic wrap and refrigerate for 30 minutes or until firm. When ready to use, roll out on a lightly floured surface to 3mm thick. To make sweet shortcrust pastry, add ½ cup (80g) icing (confectioner's) sugar.

pedro ximénez sherry
Pedro Ximénez sherry, or PX, is an intensely sweet, dark dessert sherry made from the Spanish grape variety of the same name. It's available in liquor stores.

pink peppercorns
While not technically peppercorns, these dried berries still have a mild, peppery warmth to them with slightly sweet notes. Lending their pretty, rosy colour to dishes, they're perfect cracked over chicken, fish or canapés. Buy them at most supermarkets, delis and spice shops.

prosciutto
Italian ham that's been salted and dried for up to 2 years. The paper-thin slices are eaten raw or used to lend their distinctive flavour to braises and other cooked dishes.

puffed brown rice
Whole grains of rice are heated and pressured to puff into a light, aerated cereal. Great as part of a muesli blend or baked into treats. Find them in the health food aisle of the supermarket and at health food shops.

quince jelly
Find quince jelly in the jam or relish aisles of major supermarkets, or at specialty grocers and delicatessens.

sage
A Mediterranean herb with a distinct, fragrant flavour. Commonly used in Italian cooking and often crisped in a pan with butter or oil.

sesame seeds
These small glossy seeds have a creamy, nutty flavour and can be used in savoury and sweet cooking. White sesame seeds are the most common variety, but black, or unhulled, seeds are popular for coatings in Asian cooking as well as some Asian desserts. Sesame oil is made by extracting the oil from the seeds.

shiso leaves
Sometimes called perilla, this herb comes in both green and purple-leafed varieties. It has a slight peppery flavour and can be used to wrap ingredients. The micro (baby) variety makes a pretty garnish. Find it at some greengrocers and Asian markets.

sour cherries
This book calls for both frozen and dried sour cherries. Find them, sometimes labelled as 'tart' cherries, at major supermarkets and specialty grocers.

sponge finger biscuits
Sweet and light Italian finger-shaped biscuits, also known as savoiardi. Great for desserts such as tiramisu because they absorb other flavours and soften well, yet at the same time maintain their shape. These biscuits are available in both large and small versions at supermarkets and delicatessens.

star-anise
A small brown seed cluster that is shaped like a star. It has a strong aniseed flavour and can be used whole or ground in sweet and savoury dishes. It works well in master stocks or braises.

streaky bacon
Also known as American-style bacon or belly bacon, streaky bacon is from the back end of the pork loin. Cured and smoked, it's sold in thin strips or slices and can now be found in most supermarkets and at specialty grocers.

sugar
Extracted as crystals from the juice of the sugarcane plant or beet, sugar is a sweetener, flavour enhancer, bulking agent and preservative.

brown
Light and dark brown sugars are made from refined sugar with natural molasses added. The molasses gives a smooth caramel flavour and also a soft texture. Light and dark varieties are available at supermarkets and are interchangeable.

caster (superfine)

The most commonly called for sugar in this book, caster sugar gives baked goods a light texture and delicate crumb, thanks to its fine grain. Important in many cakes as well as airy desserts such as meringues, it dissolves easily.

demerara

This sugar's large crystals, with their golden colour and mild caramel flavour, give baked goods a pronounced crust, and coffee a distinct flavour.

icing (confectioner's)

Icing sugar is granulated sugar ground to a very fine powder. When mixed with liquid or into butter or cream cheese it creates a sweet glaze or icing, plus it can be sifted over cakes or desserts. Unless specified, use pure icing sugar not icing sugar mixture, which contains cornflour (cornstarch) and needs more liquid.

raw

Light brown in colour and honey-like in flavour, raw sugar is slightly less refined than white sugar with a larger granule. It lends a more pronounced flavour and colour to baked goods. You can use Demerara sugar in its place.

white (granulated)

Regular granulated sugar is used in baking when a light texture is not crucial. The crystals are larger, so you need to beat, add liquids or heat to dissolve them.

tahini

A thick paste made from ground sesame seeds. Used in Middle-Eastern cooking and to make the dip hummus, it's available in jars and cans from supermarkets and health food shops.

vanilla

bean paste

This store-bought paste is a convenient way to replace whole vanilla beans and is great in desserts. 1 teaspoon of paste substitutes for 1 vanilla bean. Find it in small jars or tubes in the baking aisle of most supermarkets.

beans

These fragrant cured pods from the vanilla orchid are used whole, often split with the tiny seeds inside scraped into the mixture, to infuse flavour into custard and cream-based recipes. They offer a rich and rounded vanilla flavour.

extract

Syrup-like and readily available from the baking aisle of supermarkets, choose a good-quality vanilla extract, not an essence or imitation flavour.

vincotto

Translating literally as 'cooked wine', vincotto is a syrup made from grapes with a sharp, sweet-sour flavour. Use it as you would balsamic vinegar. Find it in supermarkets and specialty grocers.

vinegar

apple cider

Made from apple must, cider vinegar has a golden amber hue and a sour appley flavour. Use it in dressings, marinades and chutneys.

balsamic

Originally from Modena in Italy, there are many varieties of balsamic vinegar, ranging in quality and flavour. Aged balsamics are generally preferable. Also available in a milder white version, made with white, as opposed to red, wine.

malt

Produced from ale made from malted barley, this vinegar is typically light brown in colour. Used in pickles and chutneys, it's traditionally thought of as a natural partner for fish and chips.

rice wine

Made from fermenting rice or rice wine, rice vinegar is milder and sweeter than the vinegars made by oxidising distilled alcohol or wine made from grapes. Rice wine vinegar is available in white (colourless to pale yellow), black and red varieties from Asian food stores and some supermarkets.

white

A strong, everyday vinegar made from distilled grain alcohol.

wine

Both red and white wine can be distilled into vinegar for use in dressings, glazes, sauces and preserved condiments such as pickles. This is the vinegar to use in the classic French dressing, vinaigrette.

yeast

Dry yeast, sometimes called active dry yeast, is a granular raising agent primarily used to make dough for breads, pizzas and sweet baked treats. Buy it in sachets from the supermarket.

yoghurt

natural Greek-style (thick)

A fridge staple, natural, unsweetened, full-fat Greek-style (thick) yoghurt has multiple uses in the kitchen, from dressings to desserts. Buy it from the chilled section of the supermarket, checking the label for any unwanted added sweeteners or artificial flavours.

global measures

———○———

Measures vary from Europe to the US and even from Australia to New Zealand.

metric and imperial

Measuring cups and spoons may vary slightly from one country to another, but the difference is generally not sufficient to affect a recipe. The recipes in this book use Australian measures. All cup and spoon measures are level. An Australian measuring cup holds 250ml (8 fl oz).

One Australian metric teaspoon holds 5ml, one Australian tablespoon holds 20ml (4 teaspoons). However, in North America, New Zealand and the UK, 15ml (3-teaspoon) tablespoons are used.

When measuring liquid ingredients, remember that 1 American pint contains 500ml (16 fl oz) but 1 imperial pint contains 600ml (20 fl oz).

When measuring dry ingredients, add the ingredient loosely to the cup and level with a knife. Don't tap or shake to compact the ingredient unless the recipe requests 'firmly packed'.

liquids and solids

———○———

Measuring cups, spoons and a set of scales are great assets in the kitchen.

liquids

cup	metric	imperial
⅛ cup	30ml	1 fl oz
¼ cup	60ml	2 fl oz
⅓ cup	80ml	2½ fl oz
½ cup	125ml	4 fl oz
⅔ cup	160ml	5 fl oz
¾ cup	180ml	6 fl oz
1 cup	250ml	8 fl oz
2 cups	500ml	16 fl oz
2¼ cups	560ml	20 fl oz
4 cups	1 litre	32 fl oz

solids

metric	imperial
20g	½ oz
60g	2 oz
125g	4 oz
180g	6 oz
250g	8 oz
500g	16 oz (1lb)
1kg	32 oz (2lb)

more equivalents

———○———

Here are some equivalents for metric and imperial measures, plus varying ingredient names.

millimetres to inches

metric	imperial
3mm	⅛ inch
6mm	¼ inch
1cm	½ inch
2.5cm	1 inch
5cm	2 inches
18cm	7 inches
20cm	8 inches
23cm	9 inches
25cm	10 inches
30cm	12 inches

ingredient equivalents

almond meal	ground almonds
bicarbonate of soda	baking soda
capsicum	bell pepper
caster sugar	superfine sugar
celeriac	celery root
chickpeas	garbanzo beans
coriander	cilantro
cornflour	cornstarch
cos lettuce	romaine lettuce
eggplant	aubergine
gai lan	chinese broccoli
green onion	scallion
icing sugar	confectioner's sugar
plain flour	all-purpose flour
rocket	arugula
self-raising flour	self-rising flour
snow pea	mange tout
white sugar	granulated sugar
zucchini	courgette

oven temperatures

———○———

Setting the oven to the right temperature can be crucial when baking sweet things.

celsius to fahrenheit

celsius	fahrenheit
100°C	200°F
120°C	250°F
140°C	275°F
150°C	300°F
160°C	325°F
180°C	350°F
190°C	375°F
200°C	400°F
220°C	425°F

electric to gas

celsius	gas
110°C	¼
130°C	½
140°C	1
150°C	2
170°C	3
180°C	4
190°C	5
200°C	6
220°C	7
230°C	8
240°C	9
250°C	10

butter and eggs

———○———

Let 'fresh is best' be your mantra when it comes to selecting eggs and dairy goods.

butter

We generally use unsalted butter as it allows for a little more control over a recipe's flavour. Either way, the impact is minimal. Salted butter has a longer shelf life and is preferred by some people. One American stick of butter is 125g (4 oz). One Australian block of butter is 250g (8 oz).

eggs

Unless otherwise indicated, we use large (60g) chicken eggs. To preserve freshness, store eggs in the refrigerator in the carton they are sold in. Use only the freshest eggs in recipes such as mayonnaise or dressings that use raw or barely cooked eggs. Be extra cautious if there is a salmonella problem in your community, particularly in food that is to be served to children, pregnant women or the elderly.

useful weights

———○———

Here are a few simple weight conversions for cupfuls of commonly used ingredients.

common ingredients

almond meal (ground almonds)
1 cup | 120g
brown sugar
1 cup | 175g
white (granulated) sugar
1 cup | 220g
caster (superfine) sugar
1 cup | 220g
icing (confectioner's) sugar
1 cup | 160g
**plain (all-purpose)
or self-raising (self-rising) flour**
1 cup | 150g
fresh breadcrumbs
1 cup | 70g
finely grated parmesan
1 cup | 80g
uncooked white rice
1 cup | 200g
cooked white rice
1 cup | 165g
uncooked couscous
1 cup | 200g
cooked shredded chicken, pork or beef
1 cup | 160g
olives
1 cup | 150g

a

advent calendar stars, gingerbread 221
almond
    cranberry and nougat bark 178
    and lemon cookies 211
amaretti, prosciutto and herb stuffed
    apples 81
apple cider, mustard and sage glazed ham 34
apples
    amaretti, prosciutto and herb stuffed 81
    cinnamon and chocolate caramel 152
asparagus and feta salad 100

b

bacon
    chestnut and sage stuffing rolls 89
    wrapped spatchcocks with fig and
        herb stuffing 53
baked parsnip, sweet potato and gruyère
    mash 103
basil lavosh 105
beetroot and juniper glazed salmon with
    horseradish mash 73
biscotti
    cranberry and pistachio 211
    mixed olive and thyme 108
biscuits (savoury)
    basic parmesan 111
    basil lavosh 105
    burnt butter, honey and sage 108
    currant, juniper and blue cheese 111
    dill, rosemary and yoghurt 105
    mixed olive and thyme biscotti 108
    parmesan, fennel and lemon thyme 111
    parmesan and pink peppercorn 112
    three-cheese 111
    wholemeal poppy seed lavosh 112
biscuits (sweet)
    cranberry and pistachio biscotti 211
    ginger snaps 202
    see also cookies; shortbread; slice
black sea salt and chocolate caramel
    macarons 184
bloody mary mayonnaise 17
bombe alaska
    pandoro and vanilla 140
    raspberry and eggnog 134
bourbon, marmalade and ginger
    glazed ham 31
brandy
    custard 131
    eggnog panettone trifle 169
    jelly 169
    maple ice-cream pandoro 155
    syrup 158
bread wreath
    potato and herb 86
    raspberry sweet 143

brioche toasts: roasted pear and rosemary 95
brittle, chocolate caramel 169
broad bean, brussels sprout and almond
    salad 102
broccoli with lemon butter and thyme
    breadcrumbs 81
brussels sprout, broad bean and almond
    salad 102
burnt butter, honey and sage crackers 108
butterscotch
    peach and ginger individual panettones 124
    truffles 194
buttons, gingerbread 221

c

cake(s)
    butterscotch, peach and ginger
        individual panettones 124
    chocolate christmas cake with quince
        glaze 146
    christmas cake 116
    cranberry and fig bundt cakes with
        gingerbread antlers 121
    fig and date ice-cream cake with
        brandy syrup 158
    gingerbread cake 165
    hazelnut and brandy forest cake with
        cream cheese icing 127
    smoked almond and
        cherry panforte 146
    snowy christmas fruit cake 119
    spiced sticky date, caramel and
        star-anise cakes 121
candied pecans 133
candy cane
    and brownie ice-cream 197
    milkshakes 196
    white chocolate bars 196
caramel
    dulce de leche 230
    shortbread sandwiches 210
    swirl marshmallows 184
caramelised onion and potato stacks 100
caramels
    chewy, with salted peanuts 176
    twisted honey 181
carrots, baby, prosciutto wrapped 98
cauliflower
    caramelised onion and fontina gratin 95
    whole roasted in white wine and garlic
        butter 84
chestnut, bacon and sage stuffing rolls 89
chewy caramels with salted peanuts 176
chicken
    port and pistachio stuffed, with quince
        glaze 56
    vincotto roasted, with herb and sherry
        stuffing 53

chocolate
    caramel brittle 169
    chip gingerbread cookies 223
    christmas cake with quince glaze 146
    cookie christmas tree 224
    fudge, spiced 149
    ganache 166
    gingerbread cookie dough 217
    hazelnut pavlova with marinated
        raspberries 140
    ice-cream slice, spiced 149
    icing 218
    pecan pie bars 173
    and peppermint creams 205
    quince glaze 146
    and raspberry dipped nougat 179
    see also white chocolate
christmas cake 116
    chocolate, with quince glaze 146
    ice-cream truffles 191
    snowy 119
christmas pudding 128
christmas tree(s)
    chocolate cookie 224
    mixed gingerbread 218
    rum and raisin brownie 124
chutney: peach, chilli and rosemary 62
cinnamon
    and candied pecan pavlova 133
    and chocolate caramel apples 152
classic roast turkey with lemon
    sage butter 48
coconut
    ice: raspberry and vanilla 173
    and jam hearts 208
    and nougat slice, frozen 178
coffee
    and amaretti trifle 166
    amaretti truffles 194
    cream 166
    jelly 166
cookie garlands, gingerbread
    christmas 220
cookies
    chocolate-chip gingerbread 223
    coconut and jam hearts 208
    lemon and almond 211
    lemon and vanilla snowflakes 222
    malt 202
    spiced brown sugar 208
    see also biscuits; gingerbread
cookies and cream candy cane truffles 197
coriander and cucumber salad 76
crab
    cakes, tarragon, with aioli 18
    ricotta and tarragon stuffed zucchini
        flowers 14
crackling tips 61

cranberry
and fig bundt cakes with gingerbread
antlers 121
and pistachio biscotti 211
shortbread hearts 210
cream cheese icing 127
cream, mascarpone 161
crispy leaf potatoes with oregano salt 92
currant, juniper and blue cheese biscuits 111
custard, brandy 131

d
dill, rosemary and yoghurt biscuits 105
dips
hummus with spiced crispy chickpeas 21
minted spinach dip with yoghurt 21
tuna dip with dukkah 24
dressings and sauces
bloody mary mayonnaise 17
honey lemon dressing 103
mustard dressing 101
spiced plum sauce 65
duck fat potato and onion galette 89
duck: spice rubbed roast, with cherry sauce 56
dulce de leche 230

e
earl grey, gin and tarragon gravlax 11
eggnog truffles 191

f
fennel
roasted pork leg with baby figs and
pickled onions 68
salt 62
fig
and date ice-cream cake with brandy
syrup 158
and herb stuffing 53
fish and seafood
beetroot and juniper glazed salmon
with horseradish mash 73
crab, ricotta and tarragon stuffed
zucchini flowers 14
earl grey, gin and tarragon gravlax 11
ginger, soy and mirin oysters 18
grilled lobster with taramasalata butter 70
portuguese-style barbecued seafood
platter 73
prawns with bloody mary mayonnaise
and celery salt 17
rosemary salt baked whole snapper 76
smoky barbecued prawns 14
spicy tabasco lobster sliders 17
steamed snapper with coriander and
cucumber salad 76
tarragon crab cakes with aioli 18
see also smoked salmon

frozen coconut and nougat
slice 178
fruit cake, snowy christmas 119
fruit mince pies 187
fudge, spiced chocolate 149

g
galette: duck fat potato and
onion 89
ganache
chocolate 166
white chocolate 161
garlands
gingerbread christmas
cookie 220
gingerbread heart 222
garlic lemon butter 42, 48
ginger
brined roast turkey with pear and
potato gratin 41
snaps 202
soy and mirin oysters 18
gingerbread 181
advent calendar stars 221
antlers 218
buttons 221
cake 165
christmas cookie garlands 220
christmas trees 218
cookie dough, basic 217
cookie dough, chocolate 217
cookies, chocolate-chip 223
heart garlands 222
houses 213
men ice-cream sandwiches 152
men wreaths 220
men, salted chocolate 217
and peanut caramel squares 181
reindeer 224
sherry and caramel trifle 165
snowmen 218
glaze
chocolate quince 146
orange and maple 45
quince 56
glazed root vegetable tarte
tatin 92
gratin
cauliflower, caramelised onion
and fontina 95
pear and potato 41
gravlax: earl grey, gin and
tarragon 11
green beans with roast potatoes
and speck 101
greens with sage butter 101
grilled lobster with taramasalata
butter 70

h
ham
apple cider, mustard and sage glazed 34
bourbon, marmalade and ginger glazed 31
cheat's glazed 26
juniper, blackcurrant and vincotto
glazed 31
spiced pomegranate and orange glazed 34
hazelnut and brandy forest cake with
cream cheese icing 127
herb
butter 50
and fig stuffing 53
and sherry stuffing 53
stuffing 48
honey
and almond hasselback pumpkin 84
lemon dressing 103
honeycomb 169
and caramel ice-cream trifle 158
horseradish
mash 73
potato and apple mash with crème
fraîche 102
hummus with spiced crispy chickpeas 21

i
ice-cream
cake, fig and date, with brandy syrup 158
candy cane and brownie 197
christmas cake truffles 191
honeycomb and caramel trifle 158
pandoro, brandy and maple 155
sandwiches, gingerbread men 152
slice, spiced chocolate 149
sour cherry, ginger and pistachio 155
icing
chocolate 218
cream cheese 127
meringue 134
italian meringue 140

j
jam
cheat's raspberry 201
quick raspberry 143
sour cherry 205
jelly
brandy 169
coffee 166
pedro ximénez 165
raspberry 161
juniper
and beetroot glazed salmon with
horseradish mash 73
blackcurrant and vincotto
glazed ham 31
and tarragon brined roast turkey 48

l

labne with pistachios and pomegranate 24
lemon
    and almond cookies 211
    garlic butter 42, 48
    sage butter 48
    and vanilla snowflakes 222
lobster
    grilled, with taramasalata butter 70
    spicy tabasco sliders 17

m

macarons: black sea salt and chocolate
    caramel 184
malt cookies 202
malt vinegar and bourbon sticky
    pork belly 68
maple
    and orange glaze 45
    pavlova roll with poached pears and
        brandy cream 137
    and prosciutto wrapped brined turkey
        breasts with herb butter 50
marinated raspberries 140
marshmallows: caramel swirl 184
mascarpone cream 161
mash
    baked parsnip, sweet potato and
        gruyère 103
    horseradish 73
    potato, apple and horseradish with
        crème fraîche 102
mayonnaise: bloody mary 17
meringue
    chocolate-hazelnut pavlova with
        marinated raspberries 140
    cinnamon and candied pecan
        pavlova 133
    icing 134
    italian 140
    maple pavlova roll with poached pears
        and brandy cream 137
    pandoro and vanilla bombe alaska 140
    raspberry and eggnog bombe
        alaska 134
    raspberry and peach tart 137
    raspberry swirl pavlova wreath 143
    topping 137
milkshakes: candy cane 196
mince pies, fruit 187
minted spinach dip with yoghurt 21
mustard dressing 101

n

nougat
    chocolate and raspberry dipped 179
    and coconut slice, frozen 178
    ginger and mascarpone trifles 179

o

olive and thyme biscotti 108
onion
    brie and rosemary tarts 11
    caramelised, and potato stacks 100
orange and maple glaze 45
oregano salt 92
oysters: ginger, soy and mirin 18

p

pandoro and vanilla bombe alaska 140
panettone(s)
    butterscotch, peach and ginger 124
    trifle, brandy eggnog 169
panforte: smoked almond and cherry 146
parmesan biscuits
    basic 111
    fennel and lemon thyme 111
    pink peppercorn biscuits 112
parsnip(s)
    sweet potato and gruyère mash 103
    sweet potato and thyme yorkshire
        puddings 98
    thyme and champagne roasted 78
pastry
    shortcrust 232
    spiced brown sugar 187
pâté: smoked salmon, mascarpone
    and tarragon 16
pavlova
    chocolate-hazelnut, with marinated
        raspberries 140
    cinnamon and candied pecan 133
    roll, maple, with poached pears and
        brandy cream 137
    wreath, raspberry swirl 143
pea and ricotta tartlets 19
peach
    chilli and rosemary chutney 62
    and raspberry meringue tart 137
pear(s)
    and potato gratin 41
    and rosemary brioche toasts 95
    poached 137
    stuffing 41
pecans, candied 133
pedro ximénez jelly 165
peppermint and chocolate creams 205
pistachio and cranberry and biscotti 211
plum sauce, spiced 65
poached pears 137
poached turkey breast with lemon and
    thyme gravy 36
pork
    belly, crispy, with fennel salt 62
    belly, crispy, with spiced plum sauce 65
    belly, with garlic, caramelised onion
        and quince sauce 65

belly, malt vinegar and bourbon sticky 68
    crackling tips 61
    leg, fennel roasted, with baby figs and
        pickled onions 68
    loin, roasted, with sour cherry stuffing 58
port and pistachio
    stuffed chicken with quince glaze 56
    stuffing 56
portuguese-style barbecued seafood
    platter 73
potato
    apple and horseradish mash with
        crème fraîche 102
    and caramelised onion stacks 100
    crispy leaf, with oregano salt 92
    duck fat and onion galette 89
    and herb bread wreath 86
    and pear gratin 41
    roast, with green beans and speck 101
prawns
    with bloody mary mayonnaise and
        celery salt 17
    smoky barbecued 14
prosciutto wrapped baby carrots 98
prosecco brined turkey breast with
    brussels sprouts and speck 42
pudding: christmas 128
pumpkin: honey and almond hasselback 84

q

quick raspberry jam 143
quince glaze 56
    chocolate 146

r

raspberry
    and eggnog bombe alaska 134
    jam, cheat's 201
    jam, quick 143
    jelly 161
    and peach meringue tart 137
    and shortbread slice 198
    sweet bread wreath 143
    swirl 143
    swirl pavlova wreath 143
    and vanilla coconut ice 173
    and white chocolate trifle 161
raspberries, marinated 140
redcurrant glazed roast turkey with
    crispy tarragon 45
reindeer
    gingerbread 224
    spiced vanilla 224
relish, sour cherry 61
rice paper rolls: smoked salmon and
    avocado 19
ricotta and pea tartlets 19
rocky road 176

rolled turkey with maple and bacon
    stuffing 45
rosemary salt baked whole snapper 76
rum and raisin brownie christmas
    trees 124

S

salad
    asparagus and feta 100
    brussels sprout, broad bean and
        almond 102
    coriander and cucumber 76
    zucchini with honey lemon dressing 103
salmon
    beetroot and juniper glazed, with
        horseradish mash 73
    see also smoked salmon
salt
    fennel 62
    oregano 92
salted chocolate gingerbread men 217
sandwiches: smoked salmon, wasabi
    and radish 16
sauces – *see* dressings and sauces
seafood
    platter, portuguese-style barbecued 73
    see also fish and seafood
shortbread
    hearts, cranberry 210
    and raspberry slice 198
    sandwiches, caramel 210
    sour cherry and lemon 205
shortcrust pastry 232
slice
    chocolate pecan pie bars 173
    frozen coconut and nougat 178
    gingerbread and peanut caramel
        squares 181
    raspberry and shortbread 198
sliders, spicy tabasco lobster 17
smoked almond and cherry panforte 146
smoked salmon
    and avocado rice paper rolls 19
    mascarpone and tarragon pâté 16
    wasabi and radish finger sandwiches 16
smoky barbecued prawns 14
snapper
    rosemary salt baked whole 76
    steamed, with coriander and
        cucumber salad 76
snowflakes: lemon and vanilla 222
snowy christmas fruit cake 119
sour cherry
    ginger and pistachio ice-cream tart 155
    jam 205
    and lemon shortbread fingers 205
    relish 61
    stuffing 58

spatchcocks, bacon wrapped, with fig
    and herb stuffing 53
spice rubbed roast duck with
    cherry sauce 56
spiced brown sugar
    cookies 208
    pastry 187
spiced chocolate
    fudge 149
    ice-cream slice 149
spiced crispy chickpeas 21
spiced plum sauce 65
spiced pomegranate and orange glazed
    ham 34
spiced sticky date, caramel and
    star-anise cakes 121
spiced vanilla reindeer 224
spicy tabasco lobster sliders 17
spinach dip, minted, with yoghurt 21
steamed snapper with coriander and
    cucumber and salad 76
sticky date, caramel and star-anise
    cakes, spiced 121
stuffing
    fig and herb 53
    herb 48
    herb and sherry 53
    pear 41
    port and pistachio 56
    sour cherry 58
sweet potato, parsnip and thyme
    yorkshire puddings 98

t

taramasalata butter 70
tarragon
    butter 53
    crab cakes with aioli 18
    and juniper brined roast turkey 48
tart(s), savoury
    glazed root vegetable tarte tatin 92
    onion, brie and rosemary tarts 11
    ricotta and pea tartlets 19
tart(s), sweet
    peach and raspberry meringue tart 137
    sour cherry, ginger and pistachio
        ice-cream tart 155
tarte tatin: glazed root vegetable 92
three-cheese biscuits 111
thyme and champagne roasted
    parsnips 78
trifle
    brandy eggnog panettone 169
    coffee and amaretti 166
    gingerbread, sherry and caramel 165
    honeycomb and caramel ice-cream 158
    nougat, ginger and mascarpone 179
    raspberry and white chocolate 161

truffles
    butterscotch 194
    christmas cake ice-cream 191
    coffee amaretti 194
    cookies and cream candy
        cane truffles 197
    eggnog 191
tuna dip with dukkah 24
turkey
    brined breasts, prosciutto and maple
        wrapped, with herb butter 50
    classic roast with lemon sage butter 48
    ginger brined roast with pear and
        potato gratin 41
    poached breast with lemon and thyme
        gravy 36
    prosecco brined breast, with brussels
        sprouts and speck 42
    redcurrant glazed roast, with crispy
        tarragon 45
    rolled, with maple and bacon
        stuffing 45
    tarragon and juniper brined
        roast 48
twisted honey caramels 181

V

vanilla
    snap cookie dough, basic 217
    star wreaths 223
vincotto roasted chicken with herb
    and sherry stuffing 53

W

white chocolate
    bars, candy cane 196
    ganache 161
    and raspberry trifle 161
whole roasted cauliflower in white wine
    and garlic butter 84
wholemeal poppy seed lavosh 112
wreath(s)
    gingerbread men wreaths 220
    potato and herb bread wreath 86
    raspberry sweet bread wreath 143
    raspberry swirl pavlova wreath 143
    vanilla star wreaths 223

y

yorkshire puddings: parsnip, sweet
    potato and thyme 98

z

zucchini
    crab, ricotta and tarragon stuffed
        flowers 14
    salad with honey lemon
        dressing 103

I know for a fact that Christmas came early for a few people this year – my dream team! In my studio, we've been busily tasting everything from turkey to trifle for months now (plus more gingerbread cookies than we care to count). I'm beyond grateful for their dedication. Special mention must go to the incredible Chi, creative director of this book, and to Abby, my amazing editor. At HarperCollins*Publishers*, James, Catherine, Janelle and Belinda, thank you for making this possible – I so appreciate your ongoing support. To my sponsors, Le Creuset, KitchenAid and Smeg, you truly are the best, and I'm the luckiest. Lastly, to my friends and family (especially Angus and Tom), thank you for all your love. Despite this cheeky head start, I honestly can't wait to share my Christmas with you.

○

Donna Hay is Australia's favourite and most trusted home cook, and an international food-publishing phenomenon. Donna's 28 books have sold more than 6 million copies worldwide, been translated into 10 different languages, and her television cooking shows have brought her signature style to life for viewers in more than 14 countries. In Australia, her more recent books have dominated the bestseller charts, with *Fresh and Light* (2012) selling 202,000, *the new classics* (2013) selling 160,000, *life in balance* (2015) selling 114,000 and *basics to brilliance* (2016) selling 106,000 copies to date.

Donna Hay is a household name. Her magazine has reached more than 730,000 readers, with a digital version that's been the number one of its kind in Australia. In addition, her food range is stocked in supermarkets nationally. She is also the working mum of two beautiful boys.

Books by Donna Hay include: *modern baking*; *basics to brilliance kids*; *basics to brilliance*; *life in balance*; *the new easy*; *the new classics*; *Fresh and Light*; *simple dinners*; *a cook's guide*; *fast, fresh simple.*; *Seasons*; *no time to cook*; *off the shelf*; *instant entertaining* and the *simple essentials* collection.

donnahay.com

For more of my cookbooks, plus plenty of super simple recipes for weeknights and weekends, visit donnahay.com. While you're there, you can explore my online store of beautiful homewares, gifts and hampers. Follow me on social media to keep up-to-date with my news, videos, inspiration and all the latest on my blog.

Connect with Donna on Facebook, Instagram and Pinterest

 facebook.com/donnahay   instagram.com/donna.hay   pinterest.com/donnahayhome